KINGDOM WEALTH

THE POWER TO GET IT

D0869673

APOSTLE J. VERNON DUNCAN

Trafford

Order this book online at www.trafford.com/07-2268
or email orders@trafford.com

Most Trafford titles are also available at major online book retailers.

Cover design/artwork by Liz-Ann Aguillera.

Note for Librarians: A cataloguing record for this book is available from Library and Archives Canada at www.collectionscanada.ca/amicus/index-e.html

Printed in Victoria, BC, Canada.

ISBN: 978-1-4251-5182-9

We at Trafford believe that it is the responsibility of us all, as both individuals and corporations, to make choices that are environmentally and socially sound. You, in turn, are supporting this responsible conduct each time you purchase a Trafford book, or make use of our publishing services. To find out how you are helping, please visit www.trafford.com/responsiblepublishing.html

Our mission is to efficiently provide the world's finest, most comprehensive book publishing service, enabling every author to experience success. To find out how to publish your book, your way, and have it available worldwide, visit us online at www.trafford.com/10510

 www.trafford.com

North America & international
toll-free: 1 888 232 4444 (USA & Canada)
phone: 250 383 6864 ♦ fax: 250 383 6804 ♦ email: info@trafford.com

The United Kingdom & Europe
phone: +44 (0)1865 722 113 ♦ local rate: 0845 230 9601
facsimile: +44 (0)1865 722 868 ♦ email: info.uk@trafford.com

10 9 8 7 6 5 4

This book is dedicated to my father,
the Rev. Dr. Levi Duncan,
who still in 2008 leads a vibrant ministry
at eighty-two (82) years of age,
and is yet strong in spirit, mind and body

for his great vision and the hope he instilled with-
in us as children,
particularly with inspired words such as:
"One day, one day boys," or, "Learn to think big,"
now indelibly etched in my mind:

It is this bigness of thinking that has been a
standard bearer for us through several years of
ministry and family life, and which has no doubt
helped to form the foundation for this intriguing
discourse on Kingdom wealth.

TABLE OF CONTENTS

ACKNOWLEDGEMENTS

First, I am grateful to the Holy Spirit for revealing these embedded truths in the Holy Scriptures to me.

Second, I wish to pay great homage to my wife, Joycelyn, for her vibrant spirit and entrepreneurial disposition, who, like the Proverbs 31 woman, would see a field and buy it. Thanks for your encouragement and your great initiative.

Third, thanks to our children, Simone, Verneille and Curtis, who continue to be an encouragement to us, and for whose children's children we certainly desire to leave an inheritance.

Thanks to Liz-Ann Aguillera for the cover design, and Danielle Williams, Dabrielle Nurse and Judy Harewood for editing the document.

Then, to our good friends in the ministry, Rev. Dr. Winston Cuffie and Rev. Frank Porter, for their very supportive and insightful comments, and for noting the timeliness of this work to the Body of Christ in this season, in the foreword and preface, respectively.

Finally to the pastors, leaders and the general assembly of Divine Encounter Fellowship Ministries International; thanks for rallying around this revelation and bringing it into practical dimensions in your own lives as proof producers.

FOREWORD

Approximately eight years ago, I ministered in a Convention hosted by the Divine Encounter Fellowship Ministries International, of which Apostle J. Vernon Duncan is founder and Senior Pastor. Shortly after returning to my seat, Apostle Duncan slipped an envelope into my hand. Being who I am, I "sensed" it had to do with money! (It had nothing to do with my honorarium). Naturally, therefore, I briskly opened the envelope and was most delighted to find out that I was right about *what* the contents were. I was however pleasantly wrong about *how much* – the quantum had far exceeded my expectations!

My astonishment came largely from the fact that I knew Apostle Duncan and his Ministry were at that time occupying costly rented premises, and in the process of acquiring real estate to build an expensive sanctuary. We were, at the time, also venturing into the building of the multi-million-dollar Christ Castle facility (which we have since completed with magnificence and splendour for God's glory). Apostle Duncan's simple retort (smiling confidently) at my shocked look in his direction was: "Buy some blocks, man; buy some blocks!"

The affable Apostle later indicated to me that he was simply applying a Kingdom wealth principle, relative to sowing and reaping. I realised it was his lifestyle principle and pattern. I myself was not a stranger to sowing and reaping, having seen some absolutely astounding fruits from applying similar principles. This demonstration of daring faith and bold obedience by Apostle Duncan propelled me to a more aggressive employment of the infallible wealth principles of God's Kingdom. Thanks to Apostle Duncan! By resolutely sticking with this power principle, I have seen phenomenal, mind-boggling results in **every** sphere of my life and ministry, as well as in the lives of the many thousands whom I have had the joy of pastoring, leading, mentoring and teaching. And certainly, I have continued to be inspired by very similar trends of God's glorious favour and prosperity in the life and ministry of the highly-respected Apostle J. Vernon Duncan.

This book is a must-read recipe, a map and compass to God's expansive estate of wealth for His people. It actually puts into the minds and hands of the reader the keys to the pregnant storehouses of a covenant-keeping God.

It is said that problem-solving is the most lucrative profession in the universe. Everyone has problems and big bucks are paid for solutions. But effective problem-solving requires that one first possesses an easy-to-communicate, easy-to-use approach, which one has **proven** in one's own challenges. This stellar piece of work by Apostle Duncan is just that. **It's easily one of the best that I have read**.

The absolutely skilful unravelling of extremely potent, practical revelation from traditional Scriptures, which we usually take for granted—backed up by richly powerful faith-activating real-life testimonies—compels one to assertively move into territories of holistic wealth and prosperity and completely possess one's inheritance. Clear mastery is demonstrated in doing justice to the title of the book: KINGDOM WEALTH: THE POWER TO GET IT, from the viewpoint of spiritual revelation, scholarly research and intellectual thought. The writer is very careful to maintain balance and apostolic wisdom, amid being forthright and revolutionary.

The great writing style and communication skills employed literally flood the reader with a spirit of excitement and invigorating inspiration. Its practical style gives the feel of listening to a well-informed, highly anointed speaker expounding the Word, and furnishing real-life, workable principles for accessing all-round wealth and prosperity.

Pastors, Church leaders (and even some secular minds) will find a wellspring of motivational material for self, ministry, workers and followers. Believers will find a revolutionary eye-opener which brings into their lives, a very solid, tangible pack of answers to their most burning prayers for accessing Kingdom wealth, with sure, timely manifestation.

As the author aptly puts it on page 97 of his work, "To enlarge the place of one's tent is to break out of the narrow-minded, tunnel-vision mind-set that one has confined oneself to in the past, remembering that 'the earth is the Lord's and the fullness thereof' (Ps. 24:1)... Stretch your thinking beyond what you possess at present and start thinking 'more land, more real estate, more wealth'. To put it succinctly: 'Develop a culture of expectation.'"

Take it from me, if you are ready for a wealth-and-prosperity revolution, you are ready to read study and practise the potent principles of this masterpiece.

Rev. Dr Winston Cuffie, D.Min, PhD
Founder/Senior Pastor, Miracle Ministries,
Business Executive.

PREFACE

Like an affable airplane pilot would say to his passengers as the aircraft is about to leave the ground and ascend into the troposphere: "I invite you to buckle up; we are about to takeoff." For truly as is the case with the dependable aircraft, this publication, **Kingdom Wealth- The Power to Get it,** authored by Apostle J. Vernon Duncan, is about to take you into a higher sphere of knowledge, understanding and wisdom in relation to the subject of Kingdom wealth.

The material contained in the ensuing pages is provided by a true shepherd, whose obvious aim is to ensure that every member of the universal flock, that is the Church, receives this most timely information designed to equip each one to acquire Kingdom wealth.

For indeed, the book first and foremost provides the reader with a marvelous understanding of Kingdom wealth, which the author defines as the *'super abundant provision for life that God has made available to every child of His, who has the privilege and the right to be living in the kingdom and enjoying kingdom benefits.'*

He goes on to reveal the key to the acquisition of such wealth—a person being granted by God the rights to receive and utilize the power to get it as it relates to tithing and sowing. To this end, his main reference scripture is **Deuteronomy 8:18,** one of many instances where he uses the word of God as the basis for the many revelations he provides the reader, in his effort to educate us on the subject under review.

As one reads this most awesome manual on how each believer on this planet can acquire Kingdom wealth, one cannot help but meet with the man behind the pen—the agriculturist, the spiritual teacher, the preacher, the profound man of God. These areas of his personality are all there to escort you into a really deeper appreciation of Kingdom wealth and the means by which it could be attained.

His personal testimonies are also used at times as he goes all out to ensure that you, the reader, understand fully what is being shared.

And to conclude the work, there are the Daily Power Declarations spanning the entire week – Sunday to Saturday—and the powerful revelation of "commanding your morning." These declarations are practical and are designed to empower and nurture the seeds whatever time one sows during the week.

Need I say it? This publication is a must for every believer desirous of acquiring his or her inheritance of Kingdom wealth before he or she leaves this earth and an inheritance for his or her children's children. I encourage you to read this book and be truly blessed.

Rev. Frank M. Porter
National Director
Youth for Christ- Trinidad and Tobago

1

Your Kingdom Come Your Will Be Done

A substantive dimension of the Kingdom and a
significant proportion of our heritage is wealth—
Kingdom wealth. It is an integral part of
God's covenant with His people,
both OT and NT saints

In the book of Deuteronomy, chapter 8 and verse 18, we read:

> *And you shall remember the Lord your God, for it is He who gives you the **power** to get wealth that He may establish His covenant which He swore to your fathers.*

The Hebrew word for "power" in the above verse is *koch,* and it is the key to understanding this concept of Kingdom wealth and how to get it—the pivot of the incredible revelation in this book. We will explore that word in much detail in chapter 8, but you need to read everything before and after that to get a firm grip on your heritage as an heir of God and a joint-heir with Christ.

Once we begin to consider Kingdom Wealth, we are constrained to take a closer look at the nature and provisions of the Kingdom of God. Our Lord Jesus Christ, in teaching us to pray makes one of the most profound statements in all of Scripture: "Our Father in heaven. Hallowed be your name. Your Kingdom come, Your will be done in earth as it is in heaven." This is more than just a methodology for prayer. It is also a strong prophetic admonition by Christ. The prophetic implication is strong. Christ is telling us that if we continue to pray, there would come a time when we will see the very power of the Kingdom of heaven displayed in the earth.

The implications of the above are:

(i)   The Kingdom of God and all its attendant benefits shall be established in the earth among God's people.

(ii)   That Jesus, the King of the Kingdom, would rule in the earth just as He is now ruling in heaven, "at the right hand of power" (Mk. 14:62; Ps. 110:1). This means that we as heirs of God and joint heirs with Christ will have full rights to our inheritance in the earth, since He is our testator as well as the executor of the will Himself (Heb. 9:16-17).

(iii)   That the Church, the vanguard of the heavenly Kingdom in the earth, would be able to demonstrate fully the power of the Kingdom of God.

(iv)   That the world would see the greatest display of Kingdom power and authority through the Church in these last days that it has ever seen before.

(v)   That the very glory of Christ ("all that He possesses, all that He is, His entire Kingdom") now displayed at the right hand of the Father would be passed on to the Church. By definition, part of that promised glory that will come to the earth encompasses the goods and substance of the earth itself, for Scripture says: "The earth is the Lord's and the fullness thereof, the world and they that dwell therein" (Ps. 24:1). Once our hands are clean and our hearts are pure, we are qualified to ascend into the hill of the Lord and stand in His holy place to receive the blessing from the Lord, and righteousness from the God of our salvation (Ps. 24:4-5). The prophet Isaiah also admonishes us in Isaiah chapter 1 and verse 19: "If you are willing and obedient, you shall eat the good of the land ..."

(vi)   That we the last-day members of the body of Christ would exhibit the characteristics and behavior of a people that belong to a superior Kingdom—a chosen generation, a royal priesthood, a peculiar people and a holy nation (1 Pet. 2:9).

What is so Significant about the Kingdom?

Jesus, in profiling John the Baptist, His forerunner, in Matthew chapter 11, gives some great insight into the power of the Kingdom of God. He shows first of all that John the Baptist was no ordinary man. He was not a "reed shaken by the wind," nor was he a man "clothed in soft garments," but "more than a prophet," the greatest of those born of women (Matt. 11:7-11). Then

17

Jesus makes what I consider to be one of the most profound statements in all of Holy writ, when he interjects: **"but he that is least in the Kingdom of heaven is greater than he"** (v. 11b). Amazingly, Jesus is saying that despite how great John the Baptist was, the least in the Kingdom of heaven is greater than he. What does He mean by this?

Now consider that John was robust, radical, raucous and somewhat intimidating. He was a wild man; his food was locusts and wild honey. This means that he was far from "just cool." He was a rough-neck, so to speak. The prophet Isaiah's description of him as "the voice of one crying in the wilderness" (Matt. 3:3; Lk. 3:4) depicts the nature of the man. His voice was so loud, it was the only voice needed to accomplish what God intended. He was so charismatic and persuasive that "all Judea, and all the region around the Jordan went out to him and were baptized by him ... confessing their sins" (Matt. 3:5-6).

Moreover, John the Baptist was fearless. To the Pharisees and Sadducees who came to his baptism, he declared:

> *Brood of vipers! Who warned you to flee from the wrath to come? Therefore bear fruits worthy of repentance, and do not think to say in yourselves: 'We have Abraham as our father.' For I say to you that God is able to raise up children to Abraham from these stones. And even now the*

*axe is laid to the foot of the trees. There-
fore every tree which does not bear good
fruit is cut down and thrown into the fire.*

That was the nature of John the Baptist. The
Gospel of Luke points out that among those who
flocked to the banks of the Jordan inquiring
what to do about their lives were tax collectors
and soldiers (Lk. 3:10-14). Thus he commanded
a great following. Ultimately, Jesus Himself, the
"Lamb of God who takes away the sins of the
world," came to be baptized by John (Matt.
3:13). Yet Jesus insists that the least in the
Kingdom of heaven is greater than John.

Why is this so? John was the last of the Old
Testament (OT) prophets. By virtue of this status, he was not part of that Kingdom that was
being ushered in by Christ, although as His forerunner, he was instrumental in heralding the
coming of King Jesus and that very Kingdom.
Yes, although he announced that the Kingdom
of heaven was at hand, he himself was not privileged to be part of the Kingdom. He was neither
a recipient nor participant of this Kingdom, and
yet he exhibited such menacing authority. It is
against this already formidable backdrop that
Jesus, in wanting to show how powerful the
Kingdom of heaven is, contrasted the least in the
Kingdom with the best and the greatest prophet
of the OT era, John the Baptist.

What else is Jesus saying? He is telling us
that with the coming of this Kingdom of God
comes also the establishment of a more powerful

covenant, the New Testament (NT), in which the Kingdom of God is installed on the inside of every believer in Christ (Heb. 10:16). John the Baptist lived on the fringes of this Kingdom, but the most insignificant-looking NT saint of God finds himself or herself with this Kingdom on the inside. The lowliest of us, babe or suckling, young or old in Christ, teenager or adult, once he or she is willing to fully embrace Christ and His Kingdom, will be witness to a power that is far greater than the power of John the Baptist, however formidable John's was. This is the season when we will see this phenomenon brought to its greatest fulfillment. God will get His honor from the simplest of personalities.

How do we define the concept of "kingdom"? From the mere structure of the word, one may define it as "the domain of the king," or in the case of the Kingdom of God, "the rule of God in our lives." We know that our King is an awesome God. He is omnipotent, omniscient and omnipresent. He is the supreme authority. His Kingdom is vast and all encompassing. It is mystifying and super attractive, irresistible to say the least. Jesus tells us that from the time of John the Baptist "the Kingdom of God has been preached, and everyone is pressing into it" (Lk. 16:16). Such is the power of the Kingdom of heaven; it draws every man to it that is fully exposed to it.

A substantive dimension of the Kingdom and a significant proportion of our heritage as heirs of our King is wealth—Kingdom wealth. It is an integral part of God's covenant with His people, both OT and NT saints.

Thus, one expects that by virtue of the fact that redemption history is always progressive, and that God always moves from levels of low intensity to high intensity as time progresses, the idea of God giving wealth to His people should be even more of a reality in the NT.

The Scripture says that we grow from strength to strength (Ps. 84:7); the righteousness of God is revealed from faith to faith (Rom. 1:17); or we are being changed from glory to glory (2 Cor. 3:18). Kingdom wealth is therefore for us as much as it was for the patriarchs Abraham or Isaac or Jacob. The rest of this book is dedicated to showing God's people how to tap into this divine provision.

2

The Nature of Kingdom Wealth

*That Christ may dwell in your heart through
faith, that you being rooted and grounded
in love ... may be **filled with all the
fullness of God** (Eph. 3:17-19).*

In this season, God is providing special revelation to His last-day Church, so that we could be at the cutting edge of our faith and maximize the power that is available to us. We are beginning to understand what He has in store for us so that we may experience "all the fullness of God."

What is the fullness of God? The fullness of God is not just spiritual virtues (or godliness), but also all things that pertain to our entire lives, our beings, our existence. We are learning that "His divine power has given to us all things that pertain to life and godliness" (2 Pet. 1:3). The fullness of God is all that God has, and all that God possesses—His glory—which He gives or bestows on us His heirs. This is brought out clearly in 2 Pet. 1:3: "As His divine power has given to us **all things** that pertain to life and Godliness ..." Everything we need for life is already wrapped up in us. All that is needed is for us to activate it. In other words, there is an abundance of wealth already in us; but this is only going to become a reality as we follow God's instructions to **remember** (Gk. *zakar*, or "treat as most worthy") Him in our money matters, and in turn receive the power (the right to declare) to bring it forth (Deut. 8:18).

Verse 20 of Ephesians chapter 3 is also very revealing: "Now unto Him who is able to do exceedingly abundantly above all that we may ask or think, according to the power that works in us." This verse provides us with an explanation of the nature of the fullness of God as extended to us. This fullness is described more vividly as the "exceedingly abundantly above all that we may ask or think." In other words, the power that works in us is the foundation on which God will build our wealth. Kingdom Wealth, therefore, is not an elusive target. It is available to us. It is our heritage.

What is Kingdom Wealth?

Deuteronomy 8:18 has always been one of the most fascinating verses in Scripture. We repeat it here:

> *And you shall remember the Lord your God, for it is He who gives you the **power** to get **wealth** that He may establish His covenant which He swore to your fathers.*

The Hebrew word for wealth in the above verse is *chayil,* which means *strength, efficiency, force, worth, financial or other forms of power* (Brown, Driver and Briggs). The Oxford English dictionary defines wealth as "a large amount of money, property, or possessions," "the state of being rich," "a large amount of something desirable" (10th ed., 2005). Comparatively, the Apostle Paul talks about "the depth of the riches (or wealth) both of the wisdom and knowledge of God" (Rom. 11:33). He also refers, in Eph. 1:18, to the "riches of the glory of His inheritance in the saints." Kingdom wealth is therefore more than mere money. It is a package of God's blessings that is bestowed upon His children that makes them rich in every aspect of life and carries no sorrow with it (Prov. 10:22). It is the heritage of every child of God and it should be recognized as a provision that God has indeed made for all His children.

Kingdom Wealth Defined

Thus, Kingdom wealth may be defined as:

the super abundant provisions for life that God has made available to every child of His, who has the privilege and the right to be living in the Kingdom and enjoying Kingdom benefits.

It is part of our heritage as beneficiaries of the covenant relationship with our heavenly Father. As I said before, it goes beyond just money, and covers the whole gamut of benefits that God downloads upon us, His heirs and joint-heirs with Christ (Rom. 8:17)—money, property, possessions, social, psychological and emotional well being as well as spiritual fulfillment.

Kingdom wealth is thus all encompassing; it is available to every child of God. Notwithstanding, for the purpose of this study, we will focus more on the "money, property and possessions" aspects of Kingdom wealth. The consequences and benefits derived from the application of the principles unearthed in this study, however, would certainly not be limited to the stated emphasis of this book.

Who is an heir? An heir is one who is earmarked to receive the possessions, property, or substance of his father upon the latter's death. The Oxford English dictionary defines an heir as "a person who has the legal right to inherit the property or rank of someone else on that person's death." We are described as heirs of God and joint heirs with Jesus Christ. Therefore, we have the right of access to the fullness of the earth which belongs to our Father God. The fact is that we are not only earmarked for it, but have the right to take possession of our inheritance immediately, because of what our Testator and Possessor of all things has done for us.

Our Testator Has Ensured our Heritage

A testator is a will-maker, who determines what each inheritor should receive. Normally, a testator would not be around to see the will executed. However, in the case of our "Testator," Jesus Christ, He is the only one who has ever made a will, died, then rose again from the dead to become the administrator or executor of that will (Heb. 9:16-17):

25

*For where there is a testament, there must
also of necessity be the death of the testator. For a testament is in force after men
are dead, since it has no power at all
while the testator lives.*

But Jesus is now alive again. Hallelujah! He
must have said silently to those who were cruci-
fying Him:

*Go ahead, kill me if you like, bury me, say
that I'm dead and gone, but you will see,
I'll still live on; I shall rise again, and I will
see to it that my people for whom I die get
exactly what I willed unto them.*

Isn't that simply amazing? You should be
shouting "Hallelujah"! at the top of your voice,
and jumping up to the ceiling, because this
means that no devil, no man, no one or nothing
can rob you of your inheritance in Christ.

Do you know that if we walk with God, there
is no way that we are going to receive less than
what Christ has promised for us? He has not left
the dispensing of our blessings into the hand of
anybody else but He Himself. So do not be apprehensive in making your claims concerning
your inheritance. It is free from all encum-
brances, and you can never be cheated. Hallelujah! The testator is now also the executor.

What an incredible phenomenon! The same
person who willed our possessions to us is now
in a position to distribute it to us. Wow, that's

powerful! In other words, there should be no doubt in our minds as to our rights to it. None of this is chancy stuff. Once we walk with Him, obey His will and follow His precepts and instructions (listen to the voice of wisdom), Kingdom wealth is ours. Isaiah 1:19 says: "If you are willing and obedient you shall eat the fat, the good of the land."

Our Father possesses everything. Psalm 24 declares:

The earth is the Lord's and all its fullness, the world and those who dwell therein, for he has founded it upon the seas and established it upon the waters.

If one had any questions as to whether the Father has any rights to the substance of the earth, the answer is right here in this passage— "for he has founded upon the seas and established it upon the floods." It belongs to Him! God has jurisdiction over everything in the earth. As heirs of God, we have the rights to possess it.

Moreover, every reference of God blessing His people with money and possession in Scripture is made with superlative emphasis, for example: (i) "good measure, pressed down, shaken together and running over" (Lk. 6:38); (ii) your barns shall be filled with plenty and your vats shall overflow (Prov. 3:10); and (iii) a blessing that there will not be room enough to receive it (Mal. 3:10). What else do we need to convince us that Kingdom wealth is for us?

27

3

Covenant Wealth, Another Expression for Kingdom Wealth

Is this covenant confined only to the OT?
No! It is also for NT believers.

As heirs of God, He has made a covenant of wealth with us. Again, let us look at Deut. 8:18:

*And you shall remember the Lord your God, for it is He who gives you the power to get wealth **that He may establish His covenant which He swore to your fathers.***

This type of wealth may easily be described as Covenant wealth, since it was to be used to fulfill the covenant which God swore to our patriarchal fathers. What did God swear to our fathers? This covenant is outlined in Gen. 12:2-3:

I will make you a great nation: I will bless you and make your name great; and you shall be a blessing. I will bless those who bless you, and I will curse him who curses you; and in you all the families of the earth shall be blessed.

This is the kind of provision that God has made for those who are in covenant with Him. The above Scriptural passage is the essence of the Abrahamic covenant. God says first of all: "I will bless you." This is the first dimension of the covenant. To the average person, this by itself should be quite fulfilling; it is so good to be blessed. But God goes further: "I will make you a blessing." This means that God promised to bless Abraham with excess or super-abundance of goods, far beyond his own personal needs so that others would be blessed through him. In fact, God says to Abraham some time later: "Do not be afraid Abram, I am your shield, your exceedingly great reward" (Gen. 15:1). In other words, I Myself, the "All Sufficient One," the very creator and possessor of the substance of the earth, will be your reward. Isn't that amazing? Indeed, Kingdom wealth is more than just things.

When we look at Abraham's life, we see that he had everything. He had goods, animals, servants in excess of what he needed. The Bible describes him as "very rich in livestock, in silver, and in gold" (Gen. 13:2). Furthermore, God promised Abraham: "I will bless those who bless you, and I will curse those who curse you" (vs. 3). In other words, 'You shall have My favor and others will enjoy my favor through you.' God continues: "And in you, all families of the earth shall be blessed" (v.3). So that through Abraham's life, and through the wealth, the property and the possessions he had, families of the earth were to be blessed. This was to have extended into communities and eventually into nations. That was the nature of the Abrahamic covenant.

And that is the nature of the blessing that God has for His people even now in the NT.

Is the Abrahamic Covenant Really for Us?

Is this covenant confined only to the OT? Was it only lawful for the OT patriarchs to be wealthy? Are the virtues of NT Christianity only to be found in suffering and a contented, poverty-stricken type of humility, as some have contended? Absolutely not! The Abrahamic covenant is also for NT believers. How do we know this for sure? The Bible itself demonstrates this. We can link the OT and the NT right here in order to eliminate any doubts we may have. Here is the link; it is found in Gal. 3:3-14:

> *Christ has redeemed us from the curse of the law, having become a curse for us ... that the blessing of Abraham might come upon the gentiles in Christ Jesus, that we might receive the promise of the Spirit through faith.*

Therefore, in Christ, we are no longer under curse but under blessing, Christ having become a curse for us. As we have seen so far, the "blessing of Abraham" is certainly not only in spiritual form, as some may wish to settle for it, but it also embraces every possible benefit that is due to us as heirs of God and joint heirs with Christ. As the Scripture indicates, Abraham was not only blessed spiritually, but was also rich in livestock, gold and silver.

God is saying to us in the NT:

Like Abraham, once you follow my principles, you will enjoy my favor. I will bless you to the extent that through you families of the earth shall be blessed, starting with your own families and extending to other families in your communities. Via your community outreach ministries, you will help lift the standard of living for many who are otherwise disadvantaged; you shall change their lives for good.

Now let us look at Psalm 24:1-5 in detail:

The earth is the Lord's and all its fullness, the world and those who dwell therein. For he has founded it upon the seas, and established it upon the waters. Who may ascend into the hill of the Lord? Or who may stand in his Holy place? He who has clean hands and a pure heart, who has not lifted up his soul unto vanity nor sworn deceitfully. He shall receive the blessing from the Lord and the righteousness from the God of his salvation.

Notice that there is a balance between "the blessing from the Lord" (the substance of the earth), and righteousness. Now, prosperity is always balanced and those who are seeking to be prosperous in the Kingdom of God must also be righteous. In fact, righteousness comes first: "But seek first the Kingdom of God and His righteousness, and all these things shall be added to you" (Matt. 6:33). Kingdom wealth will be added onto you as you seek the Kingdom and His righteousness first. Take careful note of where our priority must lie!

OT Principles Like Deep Sea Treasures

Indeed, some argue that the OT principles of wealth were not really for us, but for the patriarchs and the ancient community of Israel with whom God had a special relationship. However, the Holy Spirit recently revealed to me that the principles of the OT are like deep-sea treasures buried and concealed within its historical pages. Everyone knows how valuable an ancient coin, perhaps over two thousand-years old, is. Depending on what it is one could be instantly rich if one owns one of these now. Why? Because it is regarded as ancient treasure and as such would fetch a hefty sum of money. That's what the Holy Ghost is saying to us: "In the OT are buried some ancient treasures of exceedingly great value."

Such treasures must be sought out, extracted and applied to contemporary NT faith. Many of these principles are not repeated in the NT because of what they are—"ancient treasure." Thus one does not automatically walk into Kingdom wealth, but must find it through diligent investigation of the Scriptures and aggressive application of its truths.

Thus, in order to get a holistic understanding of Kingdom wealth, part of our journey would take us back into the OT to explore the principles that have been laid down there for us. We have to analyze how these principles contributed to the wealth of the patriarchs and the ancient community of believers who followed them. We would have to see how these principles still apply today, and how contemporary Christianity can maximize God's provisions for His Church. Are you willing to take the challenge?

4

Wisdom is the Master Key
to Kingdom Wealth

*I traverse the way of righteousness, in
the midst of the paths of justice, that
I may cause **those who love me** to
inherit wealth, that I may fill
their treasuries* (Prov. 8:19-21).

Now Kingdom wealth, to begin with, does not necessarily depend on the size of your salary, your level of business acumen, organizational skills, or the like. Nor is academia a prerequisite to Kingdom wealth. Such skills will certainly be needed afterwards in order to manage all the wealth that God is going to give you as you obey the voice of wisdom and walk into your wealthy place. But the concept of Kingdom wealth surpasses our human imagination. To add to its earlier definition, Kingdom wealth may also be defined as "God's exceedingly great reward to us for being faithful and obedient as we dare to follow the voice of wisdom." **Wisdom is the Master key to Kingdom Wealth.**

The Role of Wisdom

Let us turn to Proverbs chapter 8, which is regarded by many as the wisdom chapter of the Bible. In verse 12 we read: "I wisdom dwell with prudence and find out knowledge and discretion." Wisdom is concerned about one's future, and therefore searches and discovers knowledge in order to secure the same. Thus wisdom will guide us through the Scriptures and find for us all that we need to know about life. Moreover, wisdom hates evil: "Pride and arrogance, the evil way and the perverse mouth I hate" (v. 13). In other words, those who are foul-mouthed and cannot control their tongue will have a problem with wisdom and thus Kingdom wealth; wisdom does not stay close to such people. Verse 14 says: "Counsel is mine and sound wisdom, I am understanding." Thus there is a close inter-relationship between wisdom, knowledge and understanding.

Proverbs 4:7 says: "Wisdom is the principal thing." This suggests that regarding application of these three principles, wisdom is highest in rank. Yet the fundamental principle is under-standing: ... "but in all your getting, get under-standing." Understanding is the bottom line, the foundation; so that if you do not have good un-derstanding you would not be able to apply wis-dom.

What is understanding? Understanding is the capacity to comprehend and gain knowledge. Spiritual understanding comes from the Holy Spirit Himself, the Spirit of wisdom and revela-tion (Eph. 1:17).

The interrelationship that exists among wis-dom, knowledge and understanding is somewhat cyclical. While *understanding* under-girds the whole process, giving rise to *knowledge* and providing the ammunition for *wisdom* to be applied, *wisdom*, on the other hand, would have influence on *understanding* and *knowledge* as well. *Knowledge* would also have some influence on understanding and wisdom; and so on.

What are riches? Part of the prayer of the Apostle Paul in Ephesians 1:17- 20 is:

> "...the eyes of *your understanding being enlightened, that you may know what is the hope of His calling, what are the riches of the glory of his inheritance in the saints, and what is the exceeding greatness of His power toward us who believe, according to the working of His mighty power.*"

Through the Spirit of wisdom and revelation, the eyes of our understanding are opened up that we may begin to know what the hope of His calling in us is. I believe that "the riches of the glory of his inheritance in the saints" include money, property and possession, the whole gamut of it, the super-abundance of material provisions as well as the depth of wisdom and knowledge in God (Rom. 11:33).

Wisdom is Not Difficult to Acquire

The NT implies that those who ask for wisdom will receive it in abundance. James 1:5 says: "If any of you lack wisdom, let him ask of God who gives to all liberally without reproach and it shall be given to him." Those who would obtain Kingdom wealth must seek the face of God for wisdom because it is absolutely essential for getting the wealth. Wisdom says in Prov. 8:17:

I love those who love me, and those who seek me diligently will find me. Riches and honor are with me, enduring riches and righteousness.

What does Wisdom do?

Wisdom is defined as "the right use of knowledge." Thus Wisdom takes hold of knowledge and says:

It is not enough for people to be acquainted with you; you have to be applied to their situations, their finances, their plans, their circumstances.

Wisdom says further:

The riches and honor that I have with me are for those who would listen to my voice and receive my instructions.

Wisdom takes us to the zenith of it all when she says:

My fruit is better than gold, yes, than fine gold, and my revenue than choice silver. I traverse the way of righteousness, in the midst of the paths of justice, that I may cause **those who love me** to inherit wealth, that I may **fill** their treasuries (Prov. 8:19-21).

This is mind-boggling. This is clearly one of the most powerful passages of the Bible. If we can only listen to the voice of wisdom, just imagine what God would do for us!

What then should be our Attitude towards Wisdom?

If we are looking for Kingdom wealth, then we are constrained to listen to the voice of wisdom because wisdom comes loaded with honor and riches. Moreover wisdom traverses the pathway of righteousness. In other words, if we are living righteously, or faithfully walking along the pathway of righteousness, God promises that Wisdom will be appointed to encounter us somewhere along the way. Wisdom is destined to cross our path at some point in time. We must be always on guard to take advantage of what Wisdom will say to us. This will ensure that we do not miss our *kairos* moments.

Look at the sketch below depicting how wisdom traverses the pathway of righteousness. Why is Wisdom sent by God? She is sent to give instructions to Righteousness as to how to receive enduring wealth: Wisdom speaks in this manner:

The Father has sent me to you (Righteousness) on account of your faithful-

ness, consistency and purity of heart. I will give you some instructions from the word of God as to how you can secure the wealth that God has for all those who walk in you. Make sure you heed my advice. If you love me you would listen to and follow every word that I will tell you. Remember that I promised to cause those who love me to inherit wealth, enduring wealth; I will fill your treasuries.

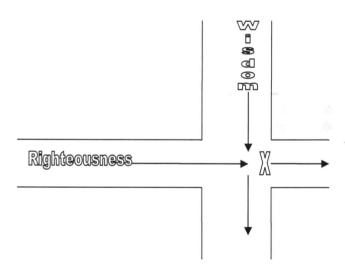

It is to be noted that wisdom traverses the pathway of righteousness; she does not as a rule follow after righteousness, or run alongside righteousness. Thus if wisdom crosses our pathway and we fail to respond to her voice on a timely basis, we would have missed our opportunity, and would have to wait for some time yet before she traverses our pathway again. So once wisdom arrives and gives her instructions, it would be strategic to respond quickly.

The Prophet Joel Supports this View

In Joel chapter 2, verses 15-26, the Lord implies that as a consequence of our solemn assemblies and righteous lifestyle, He will cause the corn, the wine and the oil to come to us; our pasture shall spring forth and our trees will begin to bear. He will cause the former rain (which he had given moderately) to combine with the latter rain in the first month. There shall be an abundance of harvest. Our barns and our threshing floors shall be full of grain and our vats shall overflow with new wine and oil, and we shall be satisfied.

In addition, all that the cankerworm, the locusts, the caterpillar and the palmerworm would have devoured, the Lord will restore. Moreover, He promises: "And My people shall never be put to shame." I elaborate more on this in chapter 9. I reiterate, God is saying that as we live a life of righteousness, and are faithful, He will always appoint Wisdom to administer our rightful reward to us—wealth and riches. Isn't that fantastic? God owns the earth, and will give its substance to those who are willing and obedient (Isa. 1:19).

The Father's Promise

I believe the Father is speaking to us in these terms:

As long as you are faithful to Me, there is no way I will leave you in lack. As My heir, and joint heir with My Son, I will bless you; I will share with you what I possess. However, you must hearken to the voice of Wisdom when she traverses your pathway, for she has come to bring enduring wealth to those who love her. Only by obeying her voice would you be able to inherit what I have in store for you.

5

Sowing and Reaping: Foundation Principles of Kingdom Wealth

Tithing is equivalent to the field preparation phase of producing a crop... tithes by itself will not bring one into Kingdom wealth, just like land preparation by itself does not bring the farmer a harvest.

Now wisdom might be the key that opens the door to our wealth, but the act of sowing is the foundation on which our Kingdom wealth is built. You cannot get Kingdom wealth if the foundation is not established and the house not built. Once the house is built, wisdom can then open the door. You cannot apply wisdom if there is no structure with which to work. Well-organized and purposeful sowing of seeds enables the professional farmer to lay the groundwork for a massive harvest. In the same way, well-planned, methodical and consistent sowing into the Kingdom of God will yield an abundance of Kingdom wealth. This is wisdom.

Sowing Techniques

The way in which one sows is critical. In the field of Agriculture, land preparation is the first stage of producing a harvest. By land preparation, the farmer indicates that he is serious about getting into the business of sowing and reaping. Thus, a good farmer would not just throw seeds in the bush and hope to get a crop; if he uses this approach, his seeds would die or, weeds will overpower them or the emerging shoots. The farmer has to be organized in his approach and use wisdom continuously if he wants a successful crop.

How much the farmer sows is also important. For example, if he prepares an acre of land, and all he sows is one little bed, all he will get are the returns from that little bed (see illustration below). Much expenditure may have gone into the exercise of land preparation, but except the entire land was covered with seeds, the farmer would not maximize his harvest.

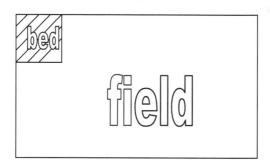

Further, having prepared his field for planting, the farmer cannot simply stand before his well-prepared field, in spite of the finely tilled soil and the expertly formed beds and drains, and speak a harvest into being. The land will never respond unless he has placed seed therein. There is a universal law that "harvest responds only to seed." As the Scripture puts it,

"While the earth remains, seedtime and harvest, cold and heat, winter and summer, and day and night shall not cease" (Gen. 8:22).

Still further, it would be an act of utter insanity for the farmer to go out into the well prepared field, simply identify some spots for watering and fertilizing and proceed to carry out these practices when there are no seeds in the ground. It is only after he has placed seed in the ground that watering and fertilizing would make sense. There is a powerful spiritual lesson here. Hereunder it is explained.

Tithing is Equivalent to Field Preparation

Tithing is equivalent to the field preparation phase of producing a crop. Tithing is an obligation and an act of obedience to God's word. As land preparation does in agriculture, your tithe indicates that you are serious about participating in the business of the Kingdom. It is the only real obligation that you have in this whole business of obtaining Kingdom wealth; the rest of your giving (your offerings, your seeding) is simply an act of wisdom. Let's examine Mal. 3:8-10 closely:

> *Will a man rob God? Yet you have robbed me. But you say, 'In what way have we robbed You?' In tithes and offerings. You are cursed with a curse, for you have robbed me, even this whole nation. Bring all the tithes into the storehouse, that there may be food in my house, and try*

me now in this, says the Lord of hosts, if I will not open for you the windows of heaven, and pour out for you such blessing that there will not be room enough to receive it.

God in the above passage charges His people for robbing Him via tithes and offerings. The penalty is drastic; they are cursed. The way to remedy the situation is to bring the tithes into the storehouse. Let me reiterate here that tithes by itself will not bring one into Kingdom wealth, just like land preparation by itself does not bring the farmer a harvest. God first told His people that they had robbed Him in tithes **and offerings**, so whatever adjustments they had to make would also involve offerings. The word "tithes," therefore, in verse 10 technically covers both. It was the understanding of the OT saints that tithes were never given without offerings. God's opening up of the windows of heaven and outpouring a superabundance of wealth upon His people could not have taken place unless there was offering or seed included with the tithes. Remember the universal law: "harvest responds only to seed."

Tithing in itself is not seed. The tithe is what we owe God, that one-tenth of our gross earnings that we are obligated to set aside for Him. Seed or offering is what God will supply to you if you do not have (2 Cor. 9:10). Follow me well, for I am going to prove this to you.

Many faithful believers claim that they diligently pay their tithes and wonder why they are not getting much in return. If you are serious about Kingdom wealth then wisdom advises that you go beyond tithing. Expecting a harvest, praying or declaring a harvest into being with only tithes is like watering or fertilizing the ground without having seed in it; it could be a frustrating exercise. One would need to explore the word of God or start "digging into the treasures of the word of God" to see what else, apart from tithes, needs be done to get Kingdom wealth.

It is said in some quarters that in the field of insurance one needs to have 100 names before one is accepted as an agent. This is the initial "price" one pays to ensure success in that field. But those names by themselves do not bring you returns. You now must make additional inputs. You must find these people and persuade them to purchase your policies. You must do something extra. Tithes and offerings function in a similar manner. If you are seriously considering Kingdom wealth, the tithe is like the initial "price" you pay to enter God's business world. Like the hundred (100) names in the insurance business, that's your prerequisite for going any further in God's business economy. Does this make sense to you?

Like in land preparation, putting your drains in and making the land look good are not enough. One could not thereafter merely wait, pray, walk through the land, prophesy to the land and expect to reap a harvest. Nothing will happen. It will never produce anything but weeds. Why? The answer is simple: "<u>Because you never put seed in the ground</u>." The harvest of Kingdom wealth demands that you add seed to your prepared land, *your tithes.* In other words, **practice sowing into you tithes.** The Holy Spirit showed me recently that the most fertile ground for sowing is not a particular name brand ministry, but surprise! surprise! "your own tithes."

"Double- tithing"—a Wisdom Move

The seeding technique of "double-tithing" is a powerful step towards Kingdom wealth. It should not merely be considered as paying tithes twice. In reality, you tithe only once. "Double-tithing," following the principle of planting the entire prepared field, in agriculture, is simply the case of matching the field that you prepared (the tithe) with a corresponding quantity of seeds (offerings). Therefore, if you prepared "an acre," so to speak, with your tithes, you would not maximize your returns unless you sow enough to cover that "acre" of tithes with your money "seed."

Like in agriculture, If you sow a small bed, that is all the returns you are going to get—the yield from a small bed. Even if a "bed" is all you can start with, your aim should be to gradually upgrade your effort so that you eventually cover the entire field. Always aspire to greater sowing. What matters is the principle, and not necessarily the great abundance of money one may give. But as fast as possible, one wants to get to the place where one's seed matches one's tithes. Continue to invest greater and greater amounts as your various harvests come in until you can do so.

The Father Supplies Seed to the Sower

What is fantastic about this system is that you do not have to worry about where the seed would come from. There is One who supplies seed. All you have to do is to become a sower by paying your tithes and getting ready to sow. Remember, you can get as much seed as you desire from this Divine Supplier, as indicated in the book of 2 Corinthians:

Now may He (the Father, the Lord of the Harvest) *who supplies seed to the sower, and bread for food, supply and multiply the seed you have sown and increase the fruits of your righteousness* (2 Cor. 9:10).

Yes, you do not need abundance of seed to begin with. All you need is an abundance of faith and a willingness to listen to the voice of Wisdom. **In fact, your biggest currency is obedience**. It's bigger than your money itself. You may have only a widow's mite to sow, but if you do it with willingness and cheerfulness, you can reap a mighty harvest. We have concrete proof of this in our ministry, where a sister in Christ, not employed, and having as little as thirty cents U.S. ($0.30), sowed it willingly and cheerfully and landed a management job paying one thousand, eight hundred and thirty-three U.S. (1,833.00) per month within one week. Her full testimony is shared later in Chapter 16.

You can start simply by asking the Father for seed. Remember what 2 Cor. 9:6 says: "He who sows sparingly will also reap sparingly" (like the little bed) "and he who sows bountifully will also reap bountifully" (like sowing the entire field). So when you ask for seed, ask big, so that you can sow into a bountiful harvest. That's how Kingdom Wealth comes—in abundance, more than enough for you and others.

Look at verse 7 of 2 Cor. 9: "So let each one give as he purposes in his heart, not grudgingly ... for God loves a cheerful giver"; this is not just tithing; this includes seeding. "Grudgingly" means "holding back," or "unwillingly." God is saying to His Body:

I do not want that 'holding-back,' stingy, and mean type of giving. I love a cheerful giver, who will purpose in his heart to give with free and open hands.

One who is pursuing Kingdom wealth enjoys giving. He or she may be faced with a bill to pay tomorrow, but knows that if what is available is not enough to meet his or her needs, then it is seed to sow, anticipating that the faithful Lord of the harvest will never disappoint His obedient children. Wisdom would suggest that one sows that which cannot meet one's need today as seed and see the bountiful returns that God will bring forth tomorrow.

A Personal Testimony

I remember on several occasions being so challenged. One Saturday morning, I realized that I needed a few thousand dollars to meet a pressing need for the following Monday morning. I did not know from where the money would have come. I was practising double-tithing at the time and was to give double tithes on that Sunday morning (the day after). The temptation then was to just give my bare tithes so that at least I would have part of that payment in my hands to make up the required sum that I so badly needed by Monday. Instead, I obeyed the Holy Spirit, stuck to the spirit of my seed covenant and did my double tithing. Needless to say, during the course of that Sunday, from several angles, the money came in abundance. I asked no one; I told no one of my situation, but people just came up to me and gave me beyond what I needed. It works! It works!

I remember another occasion, after my wife and I had been double-tithing for a few months, a sister who had not been in contact with us for over four years (that is, since she left for England) visited me in my office and said that the Lord had spoken to her while in London to bring an incredible monetary gift for us. God is no man's debtor.

Remember the Scripture says: "The earth is the Lords' and the fullness thereof" (Ps. 24:1). The Scripture also says:

> *Give and it shall be given to you: good measure, pressed down, shaken together, and running over will men put into your bosom* (Lk. 6:38).

Let us look at 2 Cor. 9:8 closely:

> *And God is able to make all grace abound toward you that you, always having all sufficiency in all things, may have abundance for every good work.*

What is grace? A simple definition is "the *unmerited* favor of God"; "*unmerited*" means you do not deserve it. Someone says that favor is unfair; that is what it would seem like in the eyes of others when God responds to your act of wisdom. Moreover, the word "*all*" in the above verse seems to suggest "unlimited" or "superabundant" provisions. The word "*always*" is also integrally linked to "*all*," suggesting that the provisions will never run out. That is the nature of Kingdom wealth; it brings abundance for every good work, abundance that never runs out. Essentially these are the words of Jesus in Jn. 10:10: "I have come that they may have life, and that they may have it more abundantly"; and in Paul: that God "is able to do exceedingly abundantly above all that we ask or think, according to the power that works in us" (Eph. 3:20) Are you ready for Kingdom wealth?

6

First Fruiting—A Most Powerful Seeding Technique

*Honor the Lord with your possessions (substance)
and with the first fruits of all your increase; so
your barns will be filled with plenty, and
your vats overflow with new
wine* (Proverbs 3:9-10)

The term "first fruits" is mentioned several times in the OT as a prominent practice of God's people. **The "first fruits" principle** is similar to the "firstling" or "first-born" principle as it pertains to offering animal sacrifices. Let us look at some Scriptural passages that address the subject matter. Notice the superabundance of returns attached to the act of "first fruiting."

In Gen. 4:3, the Scripture says Abel brought of the firstling (first-born) of his flock, and the Lord God respected Abel and his offering. This is the degree to which God honors the firstling (firstborn) or first fruit. In Num. 18:17, God instructed: "But the firstling (first-born) of a cow, the first-born of a sheep, or the firstborn of a goat you shall not redeem; they are holy."

Exodus 13:12 says:

> *...you shall set apart to the Lord all that open the womb, that is, every first born*

*that comes from an animal which you
have; the males shall be the Lord's.*

This is confirmed in Lev. 27:26:

*But the firstborn (firstling) of the animals,
which should be the Lord's first born, no
man shall dedicate; whether it is an ox or
a sheep, it is the Lord's.*

In Exod. 23:19, we read: "The first of the first
fruit of your land, you shall bring into the
house of the Lord your God."

Further, Deut. 15:19 says:

*All the first born males (Heb. zakar) that
come from your herd and your flock you
shall sanctify to the Lord your God; you
shall do no work with the firstborn (zakar)
of your herd, nor shear the firstborn (zakar) of your flock.*

What God is saying is that your firstling or
firstborn male (*zakar*) is holy unto Him.

With this in mind, let us look at Deut. 8:18
again:

*And you shall remember (Heb. zakar) the
Lord your God, for it is He who gives you
power to get wealth that He may establish
His covenant which He swore to your fathers, as it is this day.*

The word "*zakar*" here is used in the verbal sense (compare *zakar*—Gen. 1:27 "the male man"). In this context, *zakar* means "remember." Here in Deut. 8:18, it literally means "to mark, recognize or make most worthy." What God is saying to us is: "You must *zakar* or "firstling," "first fruit," or "mark, recognize or make most worthy" the Lord your God in your money matters. In other words, you must treat God as He looks at the first born male—special.

Indeed, to "firstling" or "first fruit" God in this context is to give priority to God in money matters, to give God the best of your offerings, not the leftovers, but the first and best part thereof. Exod. 23:19 says: "The first of the first fruits of your land you shall bring into the house of the Lord your God."

Another passage is 2 Chron. 31:4, 5:

> *Moreover he commanded the people who dwelt in Jerusalem to contribute support for the priests and the Levites that they might devote themselves to the Law of the Lord. As soon as the commandment was circulated, the children of Israel brought in abundance the first fruits of grain and wine, oil and honey, and of all the produce of the field, and they brought in abundantly the tithe of everything.*

Notice how particular God is about the priests and the Levites being free to devote themselves to the law of God. It is logical to see that any person making a substantial contribution to the "freeing up of the time" of the priests and the Levites would find favor with God. God is very concerned about His leaders being free to devote themselves to what they have been called to do. Leaders should not be tired and weary from seeking to make a living. They should be spending their time seeking first the face of God, the Kingdom of God and His righteousness (Matt. 6:33). The members of the local church can go a long way in ensuring this through their generous sowing into the life of the set man or woman over the house of God.

A Case in Point. The apostles in the Early Church had to delegate responsibility to seven (7) men from among the congregation to ensure that they (the apostles) were free to fulfill God's mandate on their lives (Acts chapter 6). There was some measure of confusion and much concern about the Grecian women not getting their due; everyone was coming to the apostles and complaining. The apostles ruled that the company of believers should choose from among them seven (7) men of good reputation, full of the Holy Spirit and wisdom, so that they could take care of serving tables. Consequently, the apostles would give themselves continually to prayer and to the ministry of the word (Acts 6:3-4). That is what they were called by God to do, and they were being distracted from this by other matters.

The seven (7) deacons, by taking over the serving of tables, virtually sowed into the life and ministry of the apostles. Follow the progress of two of the more well-known deacons, as a result of this act of "sowing." Steven became a man "full of faith and power," who "did great wonders and signs among the people" (Acts 6:8). Phillip went into Samaria and did great miracles; unclean spirits with loud voices came out of many who were possessed, and many who were lame and paralyzed were healed. Multitudes were converted to Christ, including Simon the sorcerer (Acts 8:6-13).

Yes, indeed, the work of five-fold ministry leadership of the Church demands that they give themselves "continually to prayer and the ministry of the word." The saints of God must be encouraged to support their leaders in this manner. Don't let them have to run about looking for money to meet the needs of their household. In fact, let the saints exercise wisdom and tap into the anointing of those who nourish them spiritually. What better way to do so than to give or to invest substantially into the life of your spiritual leader! The returns could be amazing (see next chapter).

7

A Good Strategy: Sometimes Give First Fruits Directly to Your Spiritual Leader

If we have sown spiritual things for you,
is it a great thing if we reap your
material things?

It is interesting what Bible says in Ezek. 44:30 about the benefits of bringing the first fruits directly to the priests:

> *The best of all first fruits of any kind, and every sacrifice of any kind from all your sacrifices, shall be the priest's; also you shall give to the priest the first of your ground meal,* **to cause a blessing to rest on your house.**

By giving directly to the priests, God's people in the OT caused a blessing to rest on their household. This is powerful! The principle remains the same today. Any person who would contribute to the financial welfare of their spiritual leader(s) will undoubtedly cause a blessing to rest upon his or her household.

As five-fold ministers (the NT equivalent of the priests), we should not be embarrassed to encourage our people to tap into our anointing through direct giving of their first fruits, so that their households may be blessed. This is the principle of sowing and reaping operating right here. The reason why God would bless your household is because you sowed into the life of the man of God, and by extension his household, so God, in turn, has no choice but to bless your own household; that's a spiritual law.

Church leaders must be cautioned, however, that this freedom must not be abused or misused. As we have been saying all along, the only real obligation that members of the body of Christ have in giving to God is their tithes. The rest of the giving in the Church is a wisdom thing that should be left up to the people of God to exploit once they have been given the word and desire a harvest. Leaders should not demand this, but teach the biblical principles of sowing and reaping to their people and let them decide as to the degree to which they would implement such measures. Once they see results they will continue.

NT Support

The Apostle Paul in the NT seems to support the above position when he reminds the Corinthians as well as his son Timothy: "You shall not muzzle an ox while it treads out the grain ... the laborer is worthy of his wages" (1 Cor. 9:9; Tim. 5:18). He continues in 1 Corinthians 9:11: "If we have sown spiritual things for you, is it a great thing if we reap your material things"? And then again in verses 13 and 14:

Do you not know that those who minister the holy things eat of the things of the temple, and those who serve at the altar partake of the offerings of the altar? Even so the Lord has commanded that those who preach the gospel should live by the gospel

Traditional churches and ministers have a problem of opening up certain parts of the word of God to their people, but there are principles hidden in the word of God that must be explored and practised, lest we as leaders become guilty of robbing our people from their God-given rights of blessing. One must not ignore or treat lightly opportunities for the blessing of God's people for fear of what the world may say. One cannot be apprehensive about God's method of showering blessings upon His people. True leaders pay attention to what God says, not what people say.

How is the Principle of First Fruits Applied Today?

The principle of "first fruiting" or "zakaring" God could work in several ways. Firstly, it could be viewed in terms of a first month's wage, a first week's wage, or even a first day's wage. If you consider, for example, thirty days in the month, you may divide your salary by thirty and that amount would represent a first day's wage. That may be a simple way of starting the practice of "first-fruiting." Secondly, first fruits could be the first of your increments in your new salary, or the first check in a series of payments that you expect to come to you for the next few months, or few years for that matter.

Now remember that first fruits, as a matter of wisdom, may be done in addition to your normal tithes and offering. This approach would enormously increase your power to get wealth (explained in the next chapter).

You could look at doing first fruit in the first month of the year by sowing that first month's salary into the Kingdom. It all depends on how you want to look at it, and on what Wisdom is saying to you. If you desire to start first fruiting on a small or "manageable" scale, a wise strategy would be to do it at the beginning of every month. If you want to do large first fruits, then you may do it in the first month of the year (January), or any other appropriate time of the year and see what God is going to do as a result. Based on the law of first mention, the month of January logically is a good month for first fruits, be it your first fruit of time, energy (best expressed in fasting and prayer) or money itself.

God is no man's debtor, if you follow the financial principles outlined in the Word of God, He will bring the corresponding returns because He does not disappoint. Biblical "economics" dictate that God will return to you much more than you have given. Try Him and you will see him do it. Hallelujah! I believe the most financially challenged, the poorest of believers who would come into this revelation, and practice these Biblical principles, could become wealthy right in the house of God.

If you judge your spiritual leader to be upright and worthy of his or her office as your "priest," then as often as the Holy Spirit shall lead you, practise sowing first fruit into his or her life, and watch God do marvelous things with your seed. You will never regret doing so. It is one of the most strategic sowings that one can engage in. I have seen some of the poorest people come out of their financial dilemma from this practice. I have seen children of these families blessed with scholarships and other great achievements as a result.

8

The Power to Get Wealth

Marvelous and awesome are your works oh God;
let Your mighty power be released upon my
seed right now to bring forth an awesome
harvest; for You do awesome things

Yet again, we go back to Deut. 8:18. We will zero in on the expression "power to get wealth":

> *And you shall remember* (Heb. *zakar*) *the Lord your God, for it is He who gives you* **power to get wealth,** *that He may establish His covenant which He swore to your fathers, as it is this day.*

According to the above verse, if you *remember* the Lord, if you *make* Him and what you are giving to Him *most worthy,* something amazing is going to happen. You will be able to access and use the **power to get wealth.** In other words, God will say to us: "You do not qualify to use the 'power to get wealth' unless you treat me special and make giving to me a *most worthy* exercise, just like how a firstborn male is treated by me."

Notice that God will give us the **power** to get wealth, not necessarily the wealth itself. We are the ones to employ that power to get wealth. God always leaves us with a challenge. He gives us nothing on a platter.

The Lord spoke to me one morning while my wife and I were praying and meditating on the above scriptural passage: "Go look up that word *power* in the Hebrew; it means much more than it appears to mean on the surface." So I armed myself immediately with my Brown, Driver and Briggs Hebrew-English lexicon, my Hebrew Bible and my New King James (for comparison). I made some amazing discoveries that morning. I discovered that the word **power,** rendered by the Hebrew word **koch,** is more far-reaching in scope than I had ever envisaged. The word carries a range of eight (8) nuances. In this context, it is extremely versatile and one of the most powerful revelations that I have come across in all of Scripture on the concept of Kingdom wealth.

The essence of the revelation is that the "power to get wealth" lies mainly in the potential of the seed itself and the power of our spoken word, our declaration, the expressed power of what we utter. Notwithstanding, we have no right of access to that power unless we "remember the Lord our God." Based on the several nuances or applications of the word **koch,** there is a rich assortment of declarations available to us in utilizing the "power to get wealth."

Here are the nuances of the word "**koch**" as found in the Hebrew-English lexicon:

(a) Power conferred by God to enhance ability, efficiency or, capacity. This I believe refers to business acumen, intellect, mental or physical strength, qualities that are fundamental in acquiring and amassing wealth. It also refers to new business ideas that God would download upon us through the open heaven referred to in Malachi 3:10. The blessings which God would pour out through the "windows of heaven" are certainly not literal money currency; this would be impractical. Thus I believe that these would encompass, among other things, innovative ideas for new products and services that would be translated into revenue. As one legitimately remembers God by diligently sowing into the Kingdom, God, who cannot run out of ideas, would open heaven and release hitherto unknown business concepts to that individual. These could be in the form of a series of children's stories, a special piece of equipment or tool, a new teaching series captured on CD or book, a lucrative investment or building contract, a best-selling novel or text, and the list can go on and on. But this is not all that the word **power** embraces in Deut. 8:18. God will definitely bestow these great abilities, capacities and know-how upon His people, but there are greater supernatural dimensions to the word "power" here than meets the eye. Let us examine more closely the remaining nuances.

(b) Power as in creation. What is the language of creation: "Let there be … and there was." Once you have seeded (double-tithes, first fruits or any other type of offering with which you wish to "remember" God), you now have the **power** to declare the creative word, for example: "Let there be wealth in my house" or "money cometh to me, now." This is certainly not another of your "name-it-and-claim-it" gimmicks. What you are doing by using such words is to activate your seed and add power to it. This is the basic principle behind the **power** to get wealth. Speaking such words over your seed is equivalent to the farmer "adding power" to his seeds by watering and fertilizing them once he has planted them. If he never sowed, as we observed earlier, then watering and fertilizing would be an exercise in futility. The Lord also said to me that morning when He gave me this great revelation:

> *Once you are sowing right, start speaking money and property rather than worrying about them. I have given you creative power to get wealth. So speak money instead of worrying about it. Use the same energy that you might have used to worry to speak your wealth into being.*

(c) Power as in prophetic power. Prophesying means speaking the word of the Lord as He has given it to you. You say what the Lord says. One of the expressions or language styles of prophesying is "Thus says the Lord." That is, we must speak the word of God over our seed once we have planted. For example, "Thus says the Lord, *And God is able to make all grace abound toward me, that I, always having all sufficiency in all things, may have an abundance for every good work*" (ref. 2 Cor. 9:8). Or, one may say:

> *Now, God is able to do exceedingly abundantly above all that I may ask or think,*

65

according to the power that works in me;
therefore I prophesy exceeding abundance
over my seed right now, in the name of
Jesus (paraphrased, ref. Eph. 3:20).

Yes, we ought to do like Ezekiel in Ezek. 37, and
prophesy over every dead financial "bone" in our
lives and see them come alive. We will discuss
more of this in a later chapter.

(d) Power as in the acts of deliverance. The
language of deliverance is: "In the name of Jesus, I break generational curses over my finances; I break the spirit of poverty over my life."

(e) Power associated with wisdom. Proverbs
chapter 8 is considered the wisdom chapter of
the Bible. In verses 20 and 21 we read: "I (wisdom) traverse the way of righteousness ... that I
may cause those who love me to inherit wealth,
that I may fill their treasuries."

(f) Power associated with His works. God's
works are marvelous and awesome in our eyes
(Ps. 66:3, 5). The power to get Kingdom wealth
has something to do with the marvelous power
of God and the awesome works of God. The power to do awesome things with our seed is the
kind of power God puts in our hands when we
"first fruit" Him. God is saying to us: *I am going*
to give you the awesome power to get wealth
when you remember me. One may thus declare:
Marvelous and awesome are your works oh God;
let your mighty power be released upon my seed

right now to bring forth an awesome harvest; for you do awesome things.

(g) Power associated with God's rule over His creation. This speaks of dominion power. In other words, you are taking dominion over your situation, over every thief, every robber, and every evil spirit that has been trying to rob you of what you should have. We were actually created for dominion. Thus when we seed, when we first fruit God, our dominion power is restored. That is powerful! This allows the Lord to set us above all nations; He makes us the head and not the tail; we shall be above only and not beneath (Deut. 28:1, 13). Moreover, we shall be at the cutting edge of whatever business venture we undertake; we shall excel in our profession. That is dominion power. Here is an example of a "dominion" declaration: *I take dominion over every inhibiting spirit, every generational curse, and every thief of my finances. I declare that I shall excel in the area of finances. I shall be the head and not the tail.*

(h) Power as of the soil. This dimension of the "power to get wealth" is associated with bringing forth produce; it speaks of the power of productivity. God is saying to us:

> *I will give you productivity power once you start to tithe and first fruit me; if you put aside the best of your increase for me, I will give you power to produce. You will never be barren anymore. I will cause your ground to produce in abundance.*

You would always be fruitful, like the "Psalm 1" man. You shall be like a tree planted by the rivers of waters bringing forth your fruit in its seasons; your leaves also shall not wither and whatsoever you do shall prosper.

Pay attention to this profound revelation. Do you know that a fruit tree never bears for itself? Have you ever seen a fruit tree eating its own fruit? It always bears for someone else. That's what God wants to do with us in Kingdom wealth. God will equip us to bless other people apart from ourselves and our immediate family. That is, we would fulfill the Abrahamic covenant.

Thus we may declare:

I speak productivity over my life. I declare my seed is planted in well-irrigated soil, and it shall develop into a tree by the rivers of waters. It shall bring forth its fruit in its seasons. I command the withering of my finances to cease and that abundance of prosperity be mine now. This I claim, in the name of Jesus.

We build upon the foregoing further in our "daily power declarations" segment (Chaps. 17 to 24).

The Word "Get" Reinforces the Point

*It is He who gives you the power **to get** wealth.* If one had any doubt as to whether God is really emphasizing material possessions in

Deut. 8:18, no more doubt is left after critically examining the expression "to get," in the original Hebrew. The word **get** is rendered by the Hebrew word **ʿasa.** It literally means *to make money* or *to acquire property of various kinds.* Thus this part of the verse could be read as "For it is He who gives you the power *to make money or to acquire property of various kinds*" (paraphrased).

Wow! This is powerful and revolutionary, especially in the light of the traditional thinking in the Church that believers must remain poor and be satisfied with "just a cottage below." Tell me, what debars you, what debars me, this heir of God, from having three, four or five houses and a fleet of cars as long as we are living for God, and continue to honor Him with our tithes, our substance and with the first fruits of our increase? God wants to give us great possessions as He gave to Abraham and the patriarchs. I believe it has been Satan's ploy to keep the contemporary Church bound by a particular ideology or psychological disposition which prevents the average believer from looking positively on or appreciating great abundance of material possession or money. On the other hand, God wants to fill our treasuries, as long as we can demonstrate that we know the real purpose of wealth, that is, to fulfill God's covenant of blessing others. Are you ready for it?

9

Your Solemn Assemblies Enhance the Power to Get Wealth

*The threshing floors shall be full of wheat and
the vats shall overflow with new wine
and oil* (Joel 2:24).

After all is said and done, the initiation, accumulation and maintenance of true Kingdom wealth has much to do with our consistent observance of our solemn assemblies, for true wealth (God's superabundant blessings) is inseparable from righteousness (Ps. 24:5). According to the Psalmist, wealth consists of (a) the blessings from the Lord and (b) righteousness from the God of our salvation. The Wise man also speaks of "enduring riches and righteousness" accompanying wisdom (Prov. 8:18). The discussion in this chapter will focus on Joel chapter 2.

The prophet Joel provides us with a powerful discourse on the economic and spiritual impact of our solemn assemblies, doubtlessly against a background of sowing and reaping. He shows us the power of our solemn assemblies in generating Kingdom wealth. The Father, through the prophet, begins His admonition to His people with the words: "turn to Me with all your heart, with fasting, with weeping and with mourning" (Joel 2:12). Later, in verse 15, He describes it as a "solemn assembly." Now, one may ask, "What does a solemn assembly have to do with Kingdom wealth?" As the revelation in this chapter unfolds, we will see how relevant our solemn assemblies are to Kingdom wealth.

Your quest for wealth must be properly qualified and pursued in the context of seeking the face of God and establishing your solemn assemblies. As we saw earlier, God's Prosperity is a well-balanced process. We do not simply run away with God's blessings and forget the Blesser. Through our solemn assemblies we keep our feet on the ground, so to speak, while reaching into our wealthy place.

According to the psalmist, in order for us to get the substance of the earth, we must go into the hill of the Lord and stand in His holy place. Our hands must be clean and our hearts must be pure. The result would be that we would receive not only the blessing from the Lord (that is the substance of the earth), but also righteousness from the God of our salvation (Ps. 24:1-5). The psalmist also emphasizes that those who would receive such a combination of blessings and righteousness from God belong to the generation of those who seek the face of the Lord. That is what Joel says in essence in challenging us to establish our solemn assemblies.

What is a Solemn Assembly?

According to Joel, a solemn assembly is a time appointed by God for the gathering together of His people—pastors, elders, priests, mothers,

71

fathers, young people (married or unmarried), children and even nursing babies—for the sole purpose of sanctifying themselves with fasting and prayer, and ultimately demonstrating the superiority and dominion of our God (Joel 2:12-17). It is a time when priority is given to spiritual activities. A solemn assembly is so important to God and so beneficial to God's people that even the bridegroom and the bride, just about to be married, are called upon to give priority to the things of God in preference to their own nuptial plans (Joel. 2:16b).

It is a time of repentance, fasting, weeping and consecration of ourselves before God, a time when the ministers of God should weep between the porch and the altar (Joel 2:12, 15-16). It's a time of sacrifice, where we particularly sow seeds of time and energy. These measures, combined with our money seed, have the potential to bring forth a massive harvest. Incidentally, a solemn assembly provides the most opportune moment to sow, since your ground is well watered and conditions are perfect for sowing. Moreover, in a solemn assembly, there is a cry for God to lift the reproach from over His people so that the heathens would no longer rule over God's people and sarcastically ask: "Where is their God?" (Joel 2:17). Others will see the power of our God in what He does for us, in us and through us.

Other Benefits of the Solemn Assembly

Hereunder are some other amazing benefits from observing our solemn assemblies:

Economic Benefits

(i) *The Lord will be zealous for His land (v.18).* God shall get excited about His people. When God gets excited we expect Him to do some unbelievable things. In Isa. 62, the prophet Isaiah informs us that when we pursue God relentlessly, we shall become a crown of glory and a royal diadem in His hand. We shall become His *Hephzibah* (His delight) and our land Beulah, and God shall rejoice over us (vv. 3-5). In other words, He shall extend His favor toward us (Joel 2: 18).

(ii) *God shall send grain, new wine, oil and full satisfaction (v. 19).* This is in essence Kingdom wealth. This is simply a marvelous outcome of our solemn assembly. An abundance of grain, new wine and oil are powerful indicators of wealth, even in today's economy. No doubt that powerful combination of one's money seeds, word seeds (power declarations) and prayer/energy seeds of the solemn assembly has resulted in an exceedingly abundant harvest (Eph. 3:20).

(iii) **God will remove "the northern army" far away from his people** "into a barren and desolate land, with his face toward the eastern sea and his back toward the western sea; his stench will come up, and his foul odor will rise, because he has done monstrous things" (Joel 2:20). A solemn assembly will dispel the power of Satan and his cohorts of demons assigned to God's people. God Himself shall destroy their works and drive them away into oblivion. All the plans and schemes of that "monstrous" one against us shall be brought to naught. Satan seeks to rob us of our heritage and as long as he has access to us, he would steal, kill and destroy. An effective solemn assembly will completely immobilize or make ineffective Satan's activities and create spiritual deliverance and protection for God's people, enabling us to experience life more abundantly.

(iv) *A solemn assembly results in a springing forth of new life among God's people.* Joel tells us that the open pastures would spring forth and the trees would bear their fruit; "the fig tree and the vine yield their strength" (v. 22). The Scripture indeed says: "But those who wait upon the Lord shall renew their strength; they shall mount up with wings like eagles; they shall run and not be weary; they shall walk and not faint" (Isa.40:31). A solemn assembly has the effect of watering the dry ground and pushing forth new strength, new growth, new developments and new levels of prosperity for God's people. The psalmist echoes the same sentiments when he says: "He shall be like a tree planted by the rivers of water, that brings forth its fruit in its season, whose leaf also shall not wither; and whatever he does shall prosper" (Ps. 1:3). This speaks of productivity power, indeed.

(v) *A solemn assembly will cause an abundance of rain to come your way*. You have already been blessed with the *former rain*, characterized by scattered, intermittent showers, but look out, for your solemn assembly will cause a torrential precipitation of the *latter rain*. The latter rain will combine with the former rain in the "first month" (Joel 2:23). In other words, the effects shall be accelerated. In Leviticus 26, God promised the children of Israel that if they walk in His statutes and keep His commandments and perform them, "... then I will give you rain in its season, the land shall yield its produce, and the trees of the field shall yield their fruit. Your threshing floor shall last till the time of vintage, and the vintage shall last till the time of sowing; you shall eat your bread to the full ..." (Lev. 26:4-5). Make no mistake about it; you cannot go wrong with a solemn assembly. There is no question of your land not yielding; it shall yield so much that your harvest (represented by "your threshing floor") shall overlap "the time of vintage"; in other words, the produce of one harvest shall extend to the time of the next. That is the level of abundance that is promised to us through a solemn assembly.

(vi) *The threshing floors shall be full of wheat and the vats shall overflow with new wine and oil* (Joel 2:24). Who says God does not want to give His people wealth? Who would be convinced otherwise? This type of language puts the issue beyond doubt. God has promised "... to do exceedingly abundantly above all that we ask or even think, according to the power that works in us" (Eph. 3:20). Are you ready for Kingdom wealth?

(vii) *A solemn assembly brings about restoration of years of losses and negative returns.* Generational curses will be broken. All that Satan has swindled from God's people mainly because of their former disobedience and rebellion against God shall be restored to them. God has promised that He shall indeed restore the years that the swarming locust, the crawling locust, the consuming locust and the chewing locust have devoured (Joel 2:25).

(viii) *We shall "eat in plenty and be satisfied"* (Joel 2:26). It is interesting that we are called to fast (go without food), yet at the end we shall eat in abundance. There is always a price attached to getting God's abundance. It is not an automatic blessing. Indeed, Kingdom wealth is not brought to us on a platter; we must make it happen through our generous and timely sowing, our observance of solemn assemblies and the exercise of our rights of power to get wealth.

(ix) *He will "deal wondrously" with us.* In the final analysis, a solemn assembly will cause God's favor to be upon His people and we shall never be ashamed (Joel 2:26b).

Spiritual Benefits

Our solemn assemblies will also generate the outpouring of the Holy Spirit upon God's people. The Spiritual benefits are enormous. Here is proof that prosperity within the Kingdom of God must be well-balanced between material possessions and righteousness.

(i) ***The Father will pour out of His Spirit as a reward***, upon those who would diligently observe their solemn assemblies (Joel 2:28). That is exactly what happened to the one hundred and twenty believers in the upper room. They were in the midst of a solemn assembly when the Holy Spirit was released upon them on that dramatic day of Pentecost (Acts 1:14; 2:1-4).

(ii) ***God will bless our sons and daughters with the gifts of the spirit***. They shall all prophesy. Thus a solemn assembly will benefit the young people among us (Joel 2:28).

(iii) ***The Spirit of revelation shall be evident in both old men and young***: "Your old men shall dream dreams, your young men shall see visions" (Joel 2:28).

(iv) ***The outpouring shall come upon all God's people, regardless of their social status***: "And also on My menservants and on My maidservants I will pour out My Spirit in those days."

(v) ***The power of salvation and deliverance shall intensify***: "And it shall come to pass that whosoever shall call upon the name of the Lord shall be saved. For in Mount Zion and in Jerusalem there shall be deliverance" (Joel 2:32).

10

Obedience: One of the Biggest Currencies in Kingdom Wealth

*Behold to obey is better than sacrifice, and to
heed than the fat of rams, for rebellion is as
the sin witchcraft, and stubbornness is as
iniquity and idolatry* (1 Sam. 15:22b-23).

Let the disobedient therefore not expect anything from God, for God has already laid down the conditions for acquiring Kingdom wealth in Isa. 1:19: "If you are willing and obedient, you shall eat the good of the land; but if you refuse and rebel, you shall be devoured by the sword."

Through Moses, one of Israel's greatest leaders, God lays out a classic case for obedience in Deuteronomy chapter 28:

> *Now it shall come to pass, if you dili-
> gently obey the voice of the Lord your
> God, to observe carefully all His com-
> mandments which I command you today,
> that the Lord your God will set you high
> above all nations of the earth. And all
> these blessings shall come upon you and
> overtake you, because you obey the voice
> of the Lord your God. Blessed shall you be
> in the city, and blessed shall you be in the
> country. Blessed shall be the fruit of your
> body, the produce of your ground and the*

increase of your herds, the increase of your cattle and the offspring of your flocks. Blessed shall be your basket and your kneading bowl. Blessed shall you be when you come in, and blessed shall you be when you go out ... The Lord shall command the blessing on you in your storehouses and in all to which you set your hand ... You shall lend to many nations, but you shall not borrow (vv. 1-12)

What powerful consequences there are attached to obeying diligently and carefully what God says to us! The "come-upon me and overtake me" blessing shall surely be ours. Notice that virtually everything that you do or are engaged in shall be blessed when you obey God. The end result is that you would become a net giver (lending to many) rather than a net borrower. A similar blessing is promised in Jos. 1:8, where God admonished Joshua that if he kept the book of the law in his mouth and meditated on its content day and night, he shall observe to do all that is written therein, make his way prosperous and have good success.

As was pointed out earlier, Kingdom wealth can be realized starting with the smallest of seeds as long as there is total obedience to God's directives. I recall teaching the concept of Kingdom wealth in, of all places, Eldoret, Kenya, Africa, when the Lord spoke to me saying:

This is the message for the poor people of the world. They can eat the good of the land if they would simply be willing to listen to what I say and obey me in what I have instructed in my Word concerning money matters. The resources needed to feed a nation are all located within the geographical boundaries that I have set for that nation. The real problem is the unconfessed sins and rebellion of both the present generation and their forefathers.

Since God is an excellent planner, the foregoing fact is indisputable. Much money may not be available, but there is always an abundance of obedience that can be used; it's absolutely free. Indeed, that is what is most important in walking into Kingdom wealth. We all will be well-advised to hearken unto the voice of our God, yes, the voice of Wisdom.

Yet Obedience is only part of it

Notwithstanding, the Lord recently revealed to me that obedience is only the "second level" of a four-stage hierarchy of commitment that we are expected to make to Him in our pursuit of success. These four stages are: *sacrifice, obedience, responsibility and enjoyment.* Whether it's one's money, time, energy, abilities or any other input that one endeavors to invest in God's kingdom, the returns to such investment depend heavily on the balance that one strikes among these four levels of commitment.

Sacrifice. This is good for a start, for the decision to serve God in itself is a sacrifice. Further, the decision to give any money at all into God's work, not to mention tithes, is a further sacrifice. When one adds to this the idea of sowing seeds on a regular basis, the high level of sacrifice is inevitable. Yet sacrifice is at the lowest end of the spectrum when it comes to giving to God. If one sees giving only as a sacrifice, giving then becomes a burden and, in the eyes of God, would become a virtually fruitless exercise, for one would tend to give grudgingly and painstakingly, inviting God's displeasure in the process, "for God loves a cheerful giver" (2 Cor. 9:7).

Obedience. Indeed, to obey is better than sacrifice. Thus the act of obedience in giving takes the quality of your giving to a much higher standard—a superior order as compared to mere sacrificial giving. This is because one could be giving sacrificially yet in rebellion against God. This would bring nothing but frustration and lack of blessing from God. Many people are often heard saying things like: "I am paying my tithes, I am giving offerings and yet I don't seem to be able to see my way." What is the reason for this? One of the main reasons is that such persons may not have been giving in obedience to specifically what God has been instructing them. The basic act of obedience in money matters in the Kingdom of God is paying one's tithes, as was pointed out in an earlier chapter. If one presumes on God and decides that one would give a "big" offering instead, one is likely not to see any real harvest since one is walking in disobedience to God. This is because tithing is an obligation for every believer in Christ (Mal. 3:8-10).

Apart from one's tithes, remember that one has to now purpose in one's heart to sow seed as an act of wisdom: "So let each one give as he purposes in his heart, not grudgingly or of necessity; for God loves a cheerful giver" (2 Cor. 9:8). In sowing your seed, it is strategic to listen to the voice of God as to how much to sow. If one trains one's ear to listen carefully to what God is saying, one can either immediately sow that specific sum, once the money is available; or, one may then begin to ask God to provide that specific quantum of seed He has asked one to sow. This is in keeping with the Scriptures:

> *Now may He who supplies seed to the sower, and bread for food, supply and multiply the seed you have sown and increase the fruits of your righteousness* (2 Cor. 9:10).

In other words, there is One who supplies seed to the sower; all you have to do is to be willing and obedient.

Responsibility. One of the big problems with God's people is that we do not always treat sowing into the Kingdom of God as a personal responsibility. Many give to the church in a more opportunistic manner. That is, only whenever they believe they have enough money they would pay tithes and attempt to sow seeds. Consequently, there is no consistency in their giving.

Sowing, in other words, is only intermittent. Giving as responsibility allows one to say: "This is my baby; I am committed to it; this is my responsibility." That is the type of giving attitude that God honors and for which He rewards His people.

Giving must be shifted from the realm of the abstract and the arbitrary into the realm of the assertive and the purposeful in order for it to make any significant impact on our harvest. The giver must see himself or herself as a willing participant in the establishment of God's Kingdom, and thus make giving his or her personal concern and responsibility. This principle of personal responsibility is brought out vividly in Jesus' presentation of the tenets of His ministry in Lk. 4:18:

> *The Spirit of the Lord is upon* **Me**, *because He has anointed* **Me** *to preach the gospel to the poor; He has sent* **Me** *to heal the brokenhearted; to proclaim liberty to the captives, and recovery of sight to the blind.*

Note Jesus' personalization of His mission. Jesus knew that His father sent Him to the earth on a specific mission (Jn. 20:21). However, He also knew that if He could not translate this commission into His personal mission, there was no way He could have fulfilled His task.

Enjoyment. This is the highest level of commitment that one can exhibit in anything. If you could enjoy what you do, half the burden of doing it is already removed. When one enjoys sowing into the Kingdom, this practice becomes one of absolute freedom; all the burdens surrounding this act which the average person may experience become non-existence in such a generous giver. There is no stinginess or hesitation in such giving. At this level, cheerfulness characterizes one's giving, the very attitude that delights God. It would not be difficult then for one to give generously to the church, to the poor, or to one's community. In the process, one would inevitably open up the door to massive harvests and God's bestowment of wealth. Remember that joy is a Kingdom principle: "The Kingdom of God is ... righteousness and peace and joy in the Holy Spirit" (Rom. 14:17).

It was Nehemiah who said: "for the joy of the Lord is your strength" (Neh. 8:10). Indeed, the strength that one needs in order to be consistent in sacrificial, obedient and responsible giving, can be found when one is operating at the highest level of relationship with God—at the level of joy. The prophet Isaiah declares: "Therefore with joy will I draw water from the wells of salvation" (Isa. 12:3). That's how we ought to live.

11

"Don't Stand in the Line: Sit at My Table," Says the Lord

Seek ye first the Kingdom of God and His
righteousness and all these things
shall be added to you (Matt. 6:33)

While meditating on Matthew chapter 6 and verses 25 to 33 recently, the Lord used the analogy of a typical wedding reception to illustrate a serious mistake being made by many believers. God is saying:

Many of my children are wasting a lot of time standing in the line, instead of sitting at My table and engaging in Kingdom matters. This approach is causing countless numbers of my servants to deprive themselves of their God-given heritage. Consequently, the wealth and possession that they are supposed to have they do not have.

In most wedding receptions, there are usually two sets of people being served. One set of people consists of very special guests, those who are seated at the head table with the bride and groom, and are served where they are seated. The other set is comprised of those who are asked to stand in the serving line, buffet-style, to receive their servings. The first group can relax and know that they will be served, because someone has been appointed to serve them. Special care and attention is paid to them because of their privileged status. Who are these people typically? Apart from the bride and groom, there are: the chief and other bridesmaids, the head groomsman and the other groomsmen, the fathers and mothers of the bride and the groom, the Pastor and his family, special dignitaries invited to the wedding and significant others.

Because someone has been designated to serve them, the people belonging to the first group do not have to spend time and energy in getting their meals. Consequently, they can deal with other matters. Some can catch up on old times. Others have more time to get to know one another around the table, and so on. Most importantly, there is no waiting in line; all enjoy the privileges afforded to special guests.

On the other hand, those standing in the line (no discredit meant, used only to demonstrate a spiritual lesson) utilize relatively more energy in standing, walking and waiting. On average, those in the line would receive their meals much later than those at the head table; tables are called by turns, apart from the fact that each person in the line would have to wait until all those who are standing in front of him or her are served.

What is the Spiritual Significance of all This?

God's message to us here is very strong:

(i)   "My people do not realize that there is no need to stand in line to receive their heritage, that which is already theirs; they ought to remain seated at My table; I have already designated someone to serve them.

(ii)   If My people would spend more time at my table, rather than running around looking for that which is already theirs, My blessings on their lives would not appear to be so elusive and distant.

(iii)   The reason why it is taking so long for many of My children to be blessed is because they are standing in the wrong place at the wrong time. They are living beneath their privilege.

(iv)   Sadly, My people operate just like the rest of the world, going after the mammon of unrighteousness, rather than waiting on Me and being occupied primarily in Kingdom matters. That is why I have admonished My people through my word: *Seek ye first the Kingdom of God and His righteousness and all these things shall be added to you* (Matt. 6:33). My people have not paid attention to this very important instruction. They are seeking everything else first before Me and My righteousness. That is why so many are struggling like they do. They are more focused on getting "things"—what to eat, what to drink, what to wear—running after the "mighty dollar" rather than Me, the source of all things.

(v)   When My people "stand in line," they engage themselves in exercises of futility. They work very hard, but never achieve much. The result is extreme frustration. Sometimes those in My Body are more frustrated than even unregenerate sinners, because when they expect certain things to happen, these things do not happen. But why is this so? Although my people are sacrificing much, they are walking in disobedience, and My word has not changed: "Behold, to obey is better than sacrifice, and to heed than the fat of rams, for rebellion is as the sin of witchcraft and stubbornness as iniquity and idolatry" (1 Sam. 15:22b, 23).

(vi)   I know all that My people need even before they ask Me, but they seem never to be in position to receive it. They are always so busy. Remember what I said in My word: *But those who wait upon the Lord shall renew their strength; they shall mount up with wings like eagles; they shall run and not be weary; they shall walk and not faint* (Isa.40:31).

(vii)   The wealth of the wicked is laid up for My people, but it will not be given to them while they "stand in the line." Only those who have disciplined themselves to sit around My table and occupy themselves first with My concerns are qualified to receive Kingdom benefits.

(viii) Do you remember the incident with Mary and Martha, and the difference in their approach to relating to My Son, Jesus? Mary sat at Jesus' feet and heard the word, whereas Martha, her sister, 'was distracted with much serving.' Notice the Scripture says that Martha was 'distracted.' She was working hard, kept very busy, but not busy in the things that mattered. Thus, she remained unfulfilled and dissatisfied. She complained to Jesus of Mary not assisting her in serving tables: *Lord do you not care that my sister has left me to serve alone? Therefore tell her to help me* (Lk. 10:40). This is the language of frustration, and self-pity. But I am not moved by My children's cry of self-pity when they are walking in the wrong place. What was My Son's reply? His response was in the form of a wake-up call to Martha:

Martha, Martha, you are worried and troubled about many things. But one thing is needed, and Mary has chosen that good part, which will not be taken away from her (Lk. 10:41-42).

Notice that Jesus describes Mary as having 'chosen the good part,' that is, sitting at His feet and hearing the word. This is what I want My people to do, rather than being distracted by the cares of this world. One of the greatest ploys of Satan is to get My children so busy doing everything else so that feeding on My word and walking in my wisdom take second place in their lives. This is a big mistake that My people make. I am not to be blamed for the lack of progress and prosperity in the lives of many of My people; not even the devil is to be blamed. They must blame themselves.

(ix) So often, I am disappointed in My people, for they are found constantly competing with their unsaved counterparts for that which has already been given to them, for the earth is mine and the fullness thereof, the world and all they that dwell therein. They cannot 'stand in the line' and hope to be blessed. If the unsaved, with whom many of My children compete, are not blessed, what makes My people think that they would be blessed standing in the same place as the unsaved stand? Remember My advice to you in Psalm 1:

> *Blessed is the man that does not walk in the counsel of the ungodly, nor stand in the way of sinners, nor sit in the seat of the scornful, but whose delight is in the Law of the Lord and in His Law he meditates day and night; he shall be like a tree planted by the rivers of waters, bringing forth its fruit in its own season; its leaves also shall not wither and whatsoever he does shall prosper*

If My people would only ascend into My hill and stand in My holy place, they would receive My blessings (Ps. 24:1-5). My children must know that I have already given to them all things that pertain to life and godliness (2 Pet. 1:3). Why do my children behave like underprivileged children?

(x)   I am calling My children to a new position. I want them to know that they do not belong in waiting lines. They need to wait at My table. They are more privileged than they think. I will never take that away from them. That is their heritage. It grieves me to see how My people live. Change your position; do not stand in the line; sit at my table and let's reason together. Let's talk about Kingdom business. Put yourself in position to get your Kingdom wealth"; thus says the Lord, your Provider.

12

Sowing as a Lifestyle

The more we sow is the heavier our prosperity
or Kingdom wealth clouds get, until they
burst and empty our blessings upon us.

In the book of Ecclesiastes, chapter 11, sowing is depicted as a lifestyle. Here is the breakdown:

Cast your bread upon the waters, for you will find it after many days (Eccl. 11:1).

We are admonished by the word of the Lord here to cast our bread on the waters; it will not be lost. In other words, one does not lose anything in giving to the Lord. God preserves it for you and returns it with great interest attached. He who sows as a lifestyle will never be without returns. There is always going to be some investment that would bring forth dividends for you.

Give a serving to seven, and also to eight, for you do not know what evil will be on the earth (Eccl. 11:2).

Be consistent in what you are accustomed giving, but if at times there is the need to give extra, fail not to do so, because one does not know what financial disaster one may be averting. Sometimes the enemy might be plotting to steal from you or embarrass you financially; the extra amount you give, no matter how small, may well be the straw that breaks your financial camel's back, so to speak.

If the clouds are full of rain, they empty themselves upon the earth (v. 3a).

The impact of consistent giving is comparable to what happens in the science of hydrology. Through this discipline, we learn that when the sun shines on the earth, water is lost from the streams, rivers, seas and the surfaces of plants into the atmosphere in the form of water vapor (a phenomenon known as evapo-transpiration). This water, however, goes through a recycling process by being formed into clouds over the earth; these clouds continue to enlarge or become heavier the more water is absorbed into them, until they finally empty themselves upon the earth (completing the hydrological cycle).

That is the picture that is being drawn for us in this verse. If we keep on sowing, what we are in fact doing is building up our "rain clouds," so to speak. The more we sow is the heavier our prosperity or Kingdom wealth clouds would get, until they empty our blessings upon us.

And if a tree falls to the south or the north, in the place where the tree falls, there it shall lie (v. 3b)

There is an old adage which says: "Where you make your bed, there you would lie." Although this saying tends to look at truth in a slightly negative sense, its principle seems to be captured in the above verse of Scripture. The twist here is that once you deposit your seed in God's soil, you have the right to expect that there will be a sure return from His Kingdom.

He who observes the wind will not sow, and he who regards the clouds will not reap. As you do not know what is the way of the wind, or how the bones grow in the womb of her who is with child, so you do not know the works of God who makes everything (vv. 4-5).

In God's economy, sowing must be governed by some other rules apart from those applicable to the form of agriculture practiced in bible times. In that system of agriculture, heavy winds would greatly affect the process of sowing seeds, mainly because of the "scattering" methodology used. On the other hand, rain would always affect the harvest process. Thus the farmer was cautious in observing the wind before he set out to sow or the clouds before he began to reap.

In God's economy, however, no such caution is necessary. While one may need to interpret in the natural the sign of the wind and the sign of the rain clouds, the same thing cannot be said concerning the Kingdom. One cannot fathom "the works of God who makes everything." Thus one's sowing must not be limited by external conditions or changing circumstances. One must not be intimidated by one's financial atmosphere when one sets out to invest in God's Kingdom. This is one time when caution can be thrown to the wind, for whatever is sown will return to you "after many days."

In the morning sow your seed, and in the evening do not withhold your hand: for you do not know which will prosper, either this or that. Or whether both alike will be good (v. 6).

This verse says it all. Sowing must be a lifestyle. One gets a synopsis here of how God's economy works. God relishes frequent investment in His Kingdom. One must seek every opportunity to sow. One's giving must not only consist of Sunday morning tithes and offerings, but also midweek service giving, sowing in rallies, conventions, foreign missions, to the poor in the neighborhood, into the lives of less fortunate people, and so on. Give God a wide range of investments with which to bring you your harvest, "for you do not know which will prosper, either this or that. Or whether both alike will be good."

In some cases, the harvest that one is reaping now may be from a seed that was sown about two months, or even a year ago; or as recent as yesterday. God reserves the right to determine which seed to respond to. What is guaranteed is that there will always be a harvest as long as one keeps on sowing.

13

Get Ready to Extend to the Right and to the Left

*"Lengthen your cords and strengthen your
stakes, for you shall expand to
the right and to the left."*

In the book of Isaiah, chapter 54, the prophet Isaiah provides even the seemingly most destitute, deprived and deficient among us with some amazing instructions—action that appears to be paradoxical in nature, given the depraved social, financial or even spiritual state in which one may find one's self. In other words, there is no bad-enough scenario that should deter the children of God from getting Kingdom wealth, as long as we consistently and diligently "remember the Lord" with our tithes and seed offerings. Isaiah advises:

> *Sing, O barren, you who have not borne!
> Break forth into singing, and cry aloud,
> you who have not labored with child! For
> more are the children of the desolate than
> the children of the married woman, says
> the Lord* (Isa. 54:1).

Hear the word of God to you:

> *All your life you might have been rejected,
> ridiculed, unproductive, empty-handed,
> having nothing to show for your struggles*

and efforts in life—yes desolate and for-
saken—yet you ought to sing as loud, as
intense and as aggressive as you possibly
can, knowing that this is not your perma-
nent position. Break forth into singing and
cry aloud with a cry of joy, a cry of con-
quest, not one of pain, sorrow or com-
plaint.

Isaiah gives as one of his rationale for his instructions: "For more are the children of the desolate than the children of the married woman"
(v. 1b). In other words, do not let what others
have achieved or now possess become a distrac-
tion from that which God has for you, for it is He
who will make you abundantly fruitful, even in
excess of what others may possess. How great is
our God!

The prophet extends his call to the barren to
take a quantum leap in faith and begin "to enlarge the place of your tent, and let them stretch
out the curtains of your dwellings" (v. 2). To enlarge the place of one's tent is to break out of the
narrow-minded, tunnel-vision mindset that one
has confined one's self to in the past, remembering that "the earth is the Lord's and the fullness
thereof" (Ps. 24:1). The curtains of one's dwellings refer to that which one possesses. Stretch
your thinking beyond what you possess at
present and start thinking "more land, more real
estate, more wealth." To put it more succinctly:
"Develop a culture of expectation." One can develop a culture for anything through the process
of thinking about that thing, then consequently

talking about that thing, and finally moving into action to do or receive that thing. A culture of prayer, a culture of worship, a culture of giving, a culture of church attendance; any culture may be developed in the same way.

"Do not spare," the prophet cautions (v. 2a). He is telling us that we should never be apprehensive or conservative about receiving blessings from the Lord, once we know the purpose for wealth. We must never be apologetic about what God has given to us already or what we anticipate Him to do for us now, for we are His rightful heirs, and joint-heirs with Jesus Himself. Kingdom wealth is our heritage. We may not have an earthly father, grandfather or god-father to pass anything unto us, but our heavenly Father is rich in houses and lands. You do not have to inherit anything from any man for Kingdom wealth to be yours. Your heavenly Father will give it to you. Further, if you have to be a blessing to your fellow-man or families of the earth, for that matter, you must possess much more than is enough for you and your family. God wants to move you from a state of "just enough" to that of exceedingly abundantly above all that you may ask or even think, according to the power that works within you (Eph. 3:21). Hallelujah!

The prophet is not yet finished. He continues: **"Lengthen your cords and strengthen your stakes, for you shall expand to the right and to the left"** (v. 2b, 3a). What amazing hope for the barren! You are to extend your faith beyond your existing boundary lines and mentally reinforce yourself in anticipation of the vast and incredible expansion that God is about to initiate in your life. Look beyond your present horizon and see hitherto unconquered territory that you are about to possess, and uncharted waters that you are about to cross. If you have no possession look out for many; if you have one house look out for several more; if you possess only one parcel of land, look out for three or four more. If your house needs repairs, get ready to renovate with all new material—no more mediocre standards. If you are looking for a motor vehicle, you need to think "showroom," not "used." There is about to come a massive paradigm shift in your life. Moreover, your children and descendants "will inherit the nations and make the desolate cities inhabited" (v.3b), for

> *a good man leaves an inheritance to his children's children, but the wealth of the sinner is stored up for the righteous (Prov. 13:22).*

Come buy "without money and without price" (Isa. 55:1b). Again the prophet admonishes God's people that we should not allow the initial lack of money to be a barrier to initiating the process of acquiring Kingdom wealth. One major requirement is to be thirsty enough for what you desire from God, and let that thirst drive you to the waters of the Lord to drink your fill (Isa. 55:1a). As we saw earlier, even if you have no seed to sow for your harvest, there is

One who supplies seed to all those who are willing and ready to sow.

The prophet further asks a pertinent question to which it would do us well to heed: "Why do you spend money for what is not bread, and your wages for what does not satisfy"? (Isa. 55:2). This is a rhetoric question that is intended to jolt the careless and self-indulgent among us into wise investment. If you are seeking abundance of wealth, you will have to invest in systems that would provide adequate returns to your investments. Do not be a spendthrift who goes about buying everything he sees. Look for opportunities for wise investment, institutions that have proven themselves to be stable and reliable, with a track record of satisfying returns (v. 2). What better institution than the Kingdom itself!

Kingdom Returns are not Based on Percentage but on "Fold" Measures

While on the topic of satisfying returns, permit me to advise that there are no more satisfying returns than the returns from Kingdom investments. Whereas, there is hardly any banking or financial institution in the world that can guarantee greater than four (4) to seven (7) percent return on investments, the Kingdom economy starts off with as much as thirty-fold returns and can get to a mind-blowing, incomprehensible hundredfold return: "some thirty-fold, some sixty, and some a hundred" (Mk.

4:20; Mt. 13:8). What is this "fold" return to which Jesus refers?

Here is wisdom. Try folding over a piece of paper on itself thirty times (if you can get that far), then sixty times, and then one hundred times, and observe the number of compartments created, or the extent to which the number of pieces multiply. Please note that the principle is not in the size of the compartments themselves, but rather in the multiplication of the number of such compartments. Amazingly, with only one "fold" of that paper, the results are already one hundred percent (100 %)—twice as many pieces. Two folds will generate four possible pieces (already 200%); three folds will generate eight pieces or four hundred percent (400 %); four folds would yield a possible sixteen pieces (800 %). Isn't this just amazing? I believe that this is the way in which God is prepared to multiply our "seed" investments in the Kingdom.

I myself tried the foregoing exercise and could only manage folding an 8" x 11.5" page six (6) times, mainly because of the physical limitations to the exercise itself. But amazingly, there were as many as sixty-four (64) little boxes appearing when the paper was unfolded—a multiplier factor of sixty-four (or an incredible increase of three thousand two hundred percent [3,200 %]) with only a six-fold return. Do we really know what a thirty-fold return is, far more a sixty or a hundredfold? It is simply mind-boggling. One is left with no doubt whatsoever that God's economy does not operate by simple percentage returns as man-made financial systems do. We can come to only one conclusion: the best place to invest our money is in the Kingdom of God. Can anyone argue against this? This is where true economic power lies, in God's economy.

The stock market will fail, but heaven's economic system cannot. Banking institutions, mutual fund markets or insurance companies depend on the state of a country's economy for their economic well being, but Kingdom returns are unencumbered by any situation. Whereas these institutions may take a substantial period of time (sometimes an entire working life time) to realize any meaningful benefits from investments, God's economy could yield its returns immediately or within the very season of the investment. You can never go wrong by investing your money, your time and your energy in the economy of the Kingdom.

14

Rise, Shine: Expect Something Awesome

The sons of foreigners shall build up your walls, and
their kings shall minister to you ... therefore your
gates shall be open continually, they shall not
be shut day or night, that men may bring to
you the wealth of the Gentiles (Isa. 60:11).

No Kingdom son or daughter must remain sitting and wondering in this hour as long as he or she is tithing and seeding. There is too much going for you to sit there and die. Isaiah, the prophet of prosperity advises: "Arise, shine for your light has come! And the glory of the Lord is risen upon you" (Isa. 60:1). Among the many benefits of this type of action is that "the abundance of the sea shall be turned to you. The wealth of the Gentiles shall come to you" (Isa. 60:5). Always bear in mind that harvest can only respond to seed, so that in the mind of Isaiah, he understands that wealth is not coming by some "name-it-and-claim-it" scheme, but as a result of a period of sowing.

According to Isaiah, our wealth shall be reflected in (i) the "multitude of camels" and "dromedaries of Midian and Ephah" that shall cover our land (Isa. 60:6); (ii) the gold and incense brought in by "those from Sheba" (v. 6); (iii) "the flocks of Kedar" and "the rams of Nebaioth" gathered unto us for the Lord's sake. This is nothing but wealth coming into the hands of God's people.

Further, our sons shall be returned to us from afar, bringing their silver and gold with them, "to the name of the Lord your God, and to the Holy One of Israel, because He has glorified you" (60:9b). We will see God's favor lavished on us when we add works to our faith and get up and move into godly action. We must create the culture of wealth by first of all thinking wealth, then talking wealth and finally acting to get wealth. That is where the rising and shining is necessary.

It does not finish there; Isaiah adds some more ingredients to the richness of God's blessings on His children:

> *The sons of foreigners shall build up your walls, and their kings shall minister to you ... therefore your gates shall be open continually, they shall not be shut day or night, that men may bring to you the wealth of the Gentiles (Isa. 60:11).*

What a promise! Simply by taking the appropriate action, the favor of God shall be bestowed upon His people. Who says God is not concerned about giving us, not just kings and nobles by the world's standard, but all of us, wealth? These are great and precious promises to God's people. We shall be the head and not the tail, even if we have no history of wealth or great possessions in our family lineage. There is definitely some truth in the statement: "Favor is unfair." How else can we unravel God's unmerited favor to His people who would hearken and would be careful to observe to do all that He has commanded them? (See also Deut. 28:1-14).

It gets even better. God has promised to bring to us the "glory of Lebanon," with its cypress, pine and box trees, in order "to beautify the place of My sanctuary; and I will make the place of my feet glorious" (Isa. 60:13). In other words, God will ensure that His house (our church buildings) would be constructed with the finest and most exquisite of materials. He wants His physical sanctuary to look beautiful and orderly, for He is a God of beauty and order. God's house must not be shabby-looking. As a standard, our homes should not look better than the house of God. We must take pride in beautifying the house of God. We must learn to give always to such a cause.

Even beyond the above, Kingdom wealth will be reflected in our enemies ('the sons of those who afflicted you") being made to come and bow before us, falling "prostrate at the soles of your feet" (Isa. 60:14). If you could just remain faithful to God, you would see this phenomenon take place before your very eyes. God shall make you an "eternal excellence" (v. 15). God shall improve on everything that you already have. Our excellent relationship with Him will positively impact on the very land of our existence:

Violence shall no longer be heard in your land, neither wasting nor destruction within your borders; but you shall call your walls Salvation and your gates Praise ... Your sun shall no longer go down, nor shall your moon withdraw itself; for the Lord will be your everlasting light, and the days of your mourning shall be ended (Isa. 60:18-20).

Get Ready to See Something Awesome

In Ps. 66, the psalmist David tells us what to do in order to see the awesome works of God. He invites us all to make a joyful shout to God, sing out the honor of His name and make His praise glorious (v. 1-2). We are to say to God: "How awesome are your works"! (v. 3).

His works are indeed awesome: "He is awesome in His doing toward the sons of men" (v. 5). During a recent solemn assembly, the Lord challenged us with the thought: "What thing do you want to see done that if it is done would be an awesome thing to you, for am I not awesome in my doings toward the sons of men"? Think of it and begin to declare those things that are not as though they were, and see that awesome thing accomplished in the name of the Lord and to His honor—be it acquisition of real estate, procuring a scholarship, getting married to the right person or experiencing a financial breakthrough?

You may not have yet experienced the blessing that you think you deserve, but, according to the psalmist, the Lord might have been testing you and refining you as silver and gold. You might have felt yourself even trapped in a net. Affliction, accusation, humiliation and all odds might have been meted out to you by your fellowmen. You might have been through the fire and through deep waters, but look out, God is about to bring you into "your wealthy place" (Ps. 66:10-12). Rise up, come and see the awesome works of your God.

15

The Real Secret Behind the Success of Jabez's Prayer

For God to bless him "indeed" and enlarge his coast,
he must have been a person who "remembered"
the Lord with his substance, for according to
Deut. 8:18, that seemed to be the standard
way for any OT saint to get
wealth from God.

The prayer of Jabez has become one of the most well-known prayers of all times:

Oh that You would bless me indeed, and enlarge my territory, that Your hand would be with me, and that You would keep me from evil, that I may not cause pain (1 Chron. 4:10).

A well-known contemporary Christian writer has carefully analyzed and developed the above passage into a type of "formula" prayer of prosperity for the Body of Christ. Millions of believers have embraced this prayer, and based on the writer's advice, have repeated the prayer every day for specific periods of time, and have realized great benefits. Many have testified of genuine financial miracles. However, others have followed the "formula" but have not found quite the same success.

Why did the prayer work for Jabez? Why did God answer? Was it the nature of the prayer? Was it the way it was structured? Does the prayer by itself have the power to release the financial miracles? Can this prayer simply be put to work and, by jingo, wealth would come? Is it an unconditional prayer? Or is there more to this prayer than meets the eye?

This author contends that Jabez did much more than prayed, for God to respond like He did to an apparently straightforward request. If one depends merely on the nature or structure of the prayer, one may be disappointed at the results, for there is a biblical standard set by God for getting what Jabez requested. Jabez acted wisely by recognizing that no one else had the answer to that overarching curse on his life, but God. But God does not simply grant the request of a person merely because that person states what he or she wants clearly and concisely. For example, the person who is living in sin and is presumptuous about his or her state, cannot expect to get the blessings requested in Jabez's prayer, however elegant the petition. That person must first repent, then become a giver or sower in God's Kingdom. Thus, this writer would like to advance that there are some other reasons (not explicit in the specific biblical passage, but evidenced in the rest of the biblical text) why God responded so generously to Jabez's prayer.

Jabez's request that God "would bless me indeed, and enlarge my territory," in particular, has to do with a desire for wealth, among other things. Now, Jabez was a member of the tribe of Judah ("praise")—1 Chron. 4:1. Thus, he must have been aware of his obligation to God as a "'tithe-paying" Israelite and a faithful giver of the wide range of offerings (seed) stipulated in the OT. Further, the fact that he was described as "more honorable than his brothers" reinforces the foregoing theory, for according to Malachi 3:8-10, God could not have regarded Jabez as honorable if he had been robbing Him in "tithes and offerings." Rather, he would have been considered "cursed with a curse."

Proverbs 3:9-10 supports the above case:

Honor the Lord with your possessions, and with the first fruits of all your increase; so your barns will be filled with plenty, and your vats will overflow with new wine

For Jabez to be considered honorable, the forgoing practice must have been an integral part of his every-day life, for God will certainly honor those that would honor Him. This author contends, therefore, that Jabez's abundant blessing must have been linked to his following all of God's instructions as laid out in the OT.

Moreover, if Jabez had not been tithing and seeding, God could not have granted him his request, for God works with the universal law of harvest: "Harvest responds only to seed," strongly implied in the Biblical truth: "While the earth remains, seedtime and harvest, cold and heat, winter and summer, and day and night shall not cease" (Gen. 8:22). Thus one would have to assume, beyond reasonable doubt, that Jabez was a cheerful giver himself for him to attract such an abundance of blessing from God. He knew how to sow seeds in God's vineyard.

Thus it seems likely that Jabez's prayer was really an act of empowerment of his many seeds that he had been planting. God gave him the power to get wealth on the grounds that he was a sower. For God to bless him "indeed" and enlarge his coast, he must have been a person who "remembered" the Lord with his substance, for according to Deut. 8:18, that seemed to be the standard way for any OT saint to get wealth from God. Jabez's prayer then accessed God's blessings on the basis that he was used to "remembering" or "first fruiting" God. If God gave Jabez wealth simply by his asking for it, then there seems to be no reason for the Bible to put so much emphasis on giving or sowing seeds to realize a money harvest. All one would have to do then is to set a figure in mind, and begin to ask God for this on a daily basis, and one should get it. But many well-meaning believers have tried this approach diligently over long periods and have not seen the desired results.

The fact is that there is a law that governs harvest and it is not likely to be overruled, not even by the Law Maker Himself. There is also a law of prayer, seen in the words that God spoke to Jeremiah: "Call to Me and I will answer you, and show you great and mighty things, which you do not know" (Jer. 33:3). These two laws work hand-in-hand. The law of harvest can be activated by the law of prayer, in that as long as seed has been sown, one's prayer would empower that seed, according to Deut. 8:18.

It must be noted, however, that the law of harvest will not work unless there is seed in the ground. On the other hand, the law of prayer by itself is unlikely to bring a money harvest. Thus, one may pray for long hours or even fast for days, and yet not see abundance if there is no seed. Certainly, one may gain other spiritual benefits from the long hours of prayer, but without the money seed, a money harvest is unlikely, for whatever a man sows, that he will also reap (Gal. 6:7). If you are looking for God to expand and bless you indeed, there must be some kind of monetary or material seed involved.

Thus, Jabez's prayer should not be used as a mere formula for obtaining wealth. The reason why it has worked for some and not for others is rooted in the fact that God's response to prayer is always conditional. We have already shown that merely "naming and claiming" wealth is not the way to go for obtaining true Kingdom wealth. That approach has never worked. Wherever believers have received Kingdom wealth, the foundation has always been seed.

We have already demonstrated that the only conditions under which prayer or declarative pronouncements would result in a monetary harvest is when that prayer or declaration backs up the act of sowing. That is the essence of

Deut. 8:18. No doubt Jabez would have known this, being an honorable OT character himself, and would have been fully aware that he could not have gone to God to ask such favors unless he had been a tither and a giver of offerings, as required by law.

16

Incredible Testimonies

The company called a few days later and told her that
she had been hired at an incredible salary of eleven
thousand dollars ($11, 000.00) per month

Testimony #1

A Woman who sowed
only U.S. thirty cents

I received an unbelievable miracle after I obeyed the instructions from the Lord to sow all that I had.

It was in the month of July, 2006, when the Lord led my pastor to challenge the congregation to a "special Kingdom wealth seed." This was to run over the last three weeks of the month. At the time I was not employed, and had not been working for a long time, although suitably qualified in the area of business management. Therefore, I wondered how I would participate in this exercise. The most I had in my possession on any given Sunday morning would be approximately one dollar U.S. ($1.00) or sometimes just about thirty cents (0.30) U.S. equivalent

On the second Sunday of July, the congregation was reminded of this "special Kingdom wealth seed." All I had then was ($0.30). In my mind, that did not seem to be enough to be a significant Kingdom wealth seed; I was of the opinion that one had to have much more money to get any substantial return from the Lord. I was acquainted with the Scripture which says: "He who sows sparingly will also reap sparingly and he who sows bountifully will also reap bountifully." Thus, at first I wondered whether or not I should sow what I had as my "special seed." "What can this do?" I thought for a while. Then I just simply obeyed and gave it all.

I had sent out several job applications before, but had not seen any favorable results. From the moment I sowed, I began to believe God for a job with a level of faith that I did not exercise before. I kept declaring the word of God over my seed, and for the first time I really believed that God would grant my wish. I told the Lord that I would take any salary He would offer me—seven hundred dollars U.S. ($700.00) per month, seven hundred and fifty U.S. ($750.00), or eight hundred U.S. ($800.00). God is indeed able to do exceedingly abundantly above all that we may ask or even think (Eph. 3:20).

Within a few days of obeying and sowing that seed, I got a call from a business firm to come in for an interview. Instead of one interview, I had two, then three and finally four interviews. An official of the company called me a few days later and said that they were hiring me at what was to me an incredible salary of one thousand, eight hundred and thirty-three dollars U.S. ($1833.00) per month. I was in ecstasy. For the first time in my life I knew that God was real and His promises sure.

The miracle extended even to my unsaved husband. He had been doing a gypsum trade, but not getting any significant contracts. Within the same week, he landed a contract to do eight (8) houses at a contract price of sixteen thousand U.S. ($16,000.00). What a mighty God we serve!

Testimony #2

Two Couples

As a pastor, I know of several people in our congregation who have been seeing incredible returns from sowing at every opportunity they get, at times even sowing directly into our lives (my wife and I) as their pastors. I will highlight two cases:

The first couple, over a number of years, has never failed to respond substantially to any appeal for pledges from the pulpit (according to our observations and records). Apart from this, they would always be sowing significantly into our lives as their pastors. The result is that we have witnessed tremendous economic progress in their lives over the past few years. They have recently completed their beautiful family home. They both work for the same company that just completed a massive downsizing in which a significant number of workers were paid off and retrenched. Instead of being retrenched, they were both promoted. They just acquired a brand new second family car. They continue to sow into our lives as their pastors and are moving from glory to glory and from strength to strength. God is certainly no man's debtor.

Says the wife: "It is a holistic approach that one has to adopt; your obedience to God, your relationship with Him, your lifestyle, all these add up to bring you Kingdom success."

The second couple has been giving in a similar manner as the first couple, consistently sowing into our lives as their pastors. They too have been able to complete their home. The husband was recently promoted above those who were even more qualified academically than he was. In addition, his wife recently received two sudden promotions to two levels of management within a three-year period after working for only a relatively short period in her company. In addition, in the very first promotion, she was given her own car, not without several attractive perks. This was a surprise to her not to mention several of her co-workers. But the Lord did promise that if we diligently obey the voice of the Lord our God, to observe carefully all His commandments, that the Lord our God would set us high above all nations (all people); the Lord shall make us the head and not the tail; we shall be above only and not beneath (Deut. 28:1; 13).

Testimony #3

A Christian Brother

A number of years ago I was led by the Holy Spirit to visit Divine Encounter Fellowship. At that time I had just been wrongfully dismissed from my job, precisely at the time when I had taken a substantial loan from the bank to purchase a new house. My wife at the time had also fallen ill. That night I was prophetically called out by one of our ministers and ended up being blessed with monetary gifts by the entire congregation present. I was also prayed for. A short while after, although my wife passed away, I was reinstated to my job with full pay, and all outstanding monies paid back to me retroactive to the date of my wrongful dismissal. My son also gained employment in the same firm. How marvelous is our God!

I am forever thankful to God since that time, and have continued to openly and ungrudgingly give to the Lord. God has blessed me with a new wife and I have recently built a brand new home. This is certainly not the work of a man, but the work of God, and it is marvelous in our eyes.

Testimony #4

A Christian Sister
In the month of January last year I received an increase in salary of approximately one hundred and fifty U.S. ($150.00), owing to a change in the national tax structure. Around this time, a 21-day Solemn Assembly was held at my church, Divine Encounter Fellowship, culminating in a service in which believers were asked to sow a special seed for Kingdom wealth. I de-

cided that I would give the total increment as a first fruit Kingdom seed. That Sunday night, I arrived late for church, but I hastened to the altar to lay my offering.

Some months earlier, in October of 2005 to be exact, I had visited a piece of real estate in a rural area with intent to purchase. However, I had changed my mind as I found the area to have too much of a *village* feel. Strangely, after a few months, there was a sudden, pressing desire upon my heart to own the very piece of land. I investigated and found out that the piece of land, which had been on the market for many months, was still available.

I submitted my letter of Intent to Purchase to the vendors. Soon after, they were approached by one of their close friends to purchase the said piece of land; he was offering a higher price. However, as they were bound by the agreement to me, they could only hope that I would not be able to come up with the down payment. God allowed me to make the down payment.

Ninety days after, when we met at the Attorney's office to finalize the transaction, the owners informed me that a company had approached them wanting to lease a portion of the land. I later found out from the sales-agent that they had spoken to him that very week and had been considering breaking our contract in order to capitalize on this very lucrative opportunity. However, my sales agent informed them that they would face litigation and could stand to lose much more than they could gain.

To God be the glory! I now not only own the piece of real estate, but have also successfully entered into a lease agreement for a portion of the land in the pretty attractive amount of fourteen thousand U.S. ($14,000.00) per year. In March this year, I arrived at home to meet the first check of seven thousand U.S. ($7,000.00) waiting for me. Hallelujah to the Lord most High!

I know that this financial breakthrough has been a direct result of my obedience in bringing my first fruit to the House of the Lord in January 2006, and I stand with thanksgiving before God, waiting to see what He will do next as I continue to sow into the Kingdom. Praise be to God!

Testimony #5

Another Christian Sister

When I came to Divine Encounter Fellowship, that is, about fourteen plus years ago, I was living beneath the poverty line. I was depressed and discouraged, feeling hopeless. I learned from my pastors that giving or investing in God's Kingdom was the way for us to get out of poverty. Thus I decided that that is what I would do. Thank God I did. I gave not only money, but also my time; when I did not have the money to give, I would offer my time and energy for God's service. I believed fully in the word of

God which says: "Give and it shall be given unto you, good measure, pressed down, shaken together and running over shall men give into your bosom" (Lk. 6:38).

At the time, I worked for only two hours per week and at less than two dollars U.S. ($2.00) per hour. I had a young son to support. But instead of worrying, I held on to God's word. An opportunity came for a new job, with more hours and a higher rate of pay. Then the Lord opened a door for me to study in the School of Ministry at Divine Encounter Fellowship. I graduated with a certificate in Ministerial Studies. At the same time, I continued with other studies, and successfully completed some of the other high school courses that I did not complete when my studies were previously interrupted. Those successes gave me the incentive to do even further studies. God miraculously opened the door for me to get in to the University of the West Indies School of Continuing Studies in the field of Social Work. My qualifications from there then opened the door to doing a Bachelor of Science degree in Social Sciences at the University of the West Indies. I did so well here that I got the opportunity to do my Masters degree in Social Science.

All of this happened while I continued to sow generously into the Kingdom of God. My present job is now paying literally one thousand times the amount I was receiving when I started this road to success within the Kingdom of God. I am soon to open my own business. To God be the glory!

Wealth will not come to you if you only pray and wait, in spite of how genuine or sincere you are. You must begin to give and be faithful or consistent in your giving. If God did it for me he can do it for you too.

Testimony #6

This Author
A few years ago, God directed my wife and me to make certain investments in real estate that have suddenly escalated in value within recent times. The amazing thing about these investments is that they were made in what appeared to be lean seasons while we insisted in double and, in some cases, close to triple tithing. Like Isaac, we had learned to sow generously in famine. Now God's clock is ticking for us. In addition, God has birthed and enabled me to write several unique books that have the potential for worldwide distribution, including this present volume. God has also blessed us with a unique hair rejuvenating product which again has the potential for international distribution; it's only a matter of time. In addition, God has blessed our children with academic scholarships, and the necessary finances to see them through various phases of their academic pursuits.

God has also blessed our ministry in allowing us to acquire relatively large parcels of land that are now fully paid up and that have also amassed exponential increases in value within recent times. The first phase of a five thousand-seat church complex, our fellowship hall, has been built without having to borrow from the bank. We are now completely debt-free, and are embarking on the erection of a business center. A five-star hotel is earmarked for another parcel of land. Our five thousand-seat auditorium is next. Truly, God is no man's debtor.

Recently, the Lord challenged me, while attending an international conference in Dallas, Texas, U.S.A, to sow an incredible sum to a well-known world evangelism ministry. I immediately took up the challenge, not knowing where the money would have come from, at the same time being aware of the high exchange rate of our currency as compared to the U.S. dollar. The Lord challenged me: "Sow into your new church building, the five-thousand (5000)-seater." Within a short while, God had provided that seed. I am of the firm belief that whatever building we undertake in this season, seed is already in the ground and the harvest is already available for building it. Many of our members are experiencing great prosperity. We are on the lookout for more lands and more property, for the earth is the Lord's and the fullness thereof.

17

Daily Power Declarations

This section allows us to make our daily declarations with emphasis on a specific dimension of the "power to get wealth." Most believers do their tithing and sowing (their "remembering" of the Lord) during the Sunday morning service. That leaves them with the rest of the week to empower and nurture their seed, and, in the process, exercise the "power to get wealth."

Here is a very practical approach that one can take to ensure that every aspect of this power is adequately applied. In this book, we provide the reader with a daily guide to using the power to get wealth. Each of the seven supernatural areas of power (see chapter 8) is assigned a day (Sunday to Saturday) of the week. Thus we have: Creative Sunday, Prophetic Monday, Deliverance Tuesday, Wisdom Wednesday, Awesome Thursday, Dominion Friday and Productivity Saturday. On each day, one may confine one's declarations to the specific aspect of power represented by that day.

Remember that the power to get wealth is exhibited by your declarative word. What you say on a daily basis would determine what happens to your seed. Just like a farmer has to water his seeds on a daily basis to ensure the proper and effective nurturing of these seeds, so we as believers would have to declare the power word over our "seed" on a daily basis. You see what the farmer is effectively doing is empowering his seeds daily so that they bring forth maximum returns. He further increases this power through the application of various ingredients such as fertilizer, pesticides, foliar sprays, hormones and so on.

The next seven (7) chapters will be in the form of a brief "daily bread" type guide. Use this format to speak those things that are not as though they were. Do this with great confidence and aggression. Do not doubt. Make your declarations first thing early in the morning, and keep repeating them, either wholly or in part during the day. *Remember, specificity of expression allows for specificity of activation.* You speak what you wish to see happen. By the end of the week, you would have covered all areas of the power to get wealth. Look out for your Kingdom wealth flow as you keep on sowing and declaring. As we learned previously, the seeds that you sow during the midweek services in your church, or in other spiritually fertile ground, would further enhance your returns over and above your Sunday morning seed. The more you sow is the more seed you have to empower.

18

Creative Sunday

Taking a cue from God's creative language, today I am focusing my declarations on the power associated with creation as I pursue Kingdom wealth. The language of creation is "Let there be …" or "Let the … bring forth …" I will speak those things that are not as though they were. I am declaring that something be created out of "nothing." This is particularly relevant to those who could sow only the widow's mite (virtually "nothing"). "Can any good thing come out of my seemingly insignificant seed?" I am just going to speak the creative word and see God's creative power released on my seed.

My Declarations

In the act of creation, Lord, whatever you said, whatever you called into being, it was so (Genesis chapt. 1). You have given me the same power, now that I have remembered you with my substance. As your heir and joint-heir with Christ, I have a creative word in my mouth to speak those things that are not as though they were. Therefore, let there come forth from my seed a superabundant harvest now. I have remembered you oh Lord, therefore I have the rights to use your power to speak a creative word to my seed. Money come unto me now! Property and possession come into my hands now.

I am an heir of God. Therefore what God possesses is my heritage. I speak my heritage into being now! Spirit of the living God move upon the face of my waters, and let there spring forth from them life more abundantly. Father, let your Kingdom come, and let your will be done in my life, oh Lord, for you are able to do exceedingly abundantly above all that I may ask or even think, according to the power that works within me. Your will for your children is that we must have life more abundantly. Therefore, I ought not to have any lack whatsoever. I must have enough to give. Yes, that is Your will concerning me Oh Lord. Let men give into my bosom now, just like Your word says, and let your blessings be pressed down, shaken together and running over for me.

I also declare an abundance of souls to my account. Let souls come into Your Kingdom as a result of my personal witness, oh Lord. I must not be barren any more. Let Your creative power bring forth souls oh Lord. Lead me to those who would be ready to respond to the message of salvation and be saved. Father, I believe it's done. Thank you Lord. Amen!

19

Prophetic Monday

Today I will prophesy to my seed. I will release the ingredient of the word of God upon my seed and speak what God has said in His word concerning my prosperity. The word of God must come alive in my situation. It must not just be written in the Bible. Whatever God has said about my prosperity must come to pass today.

My Declarations

Like Ezekiel, I prophesy to every dry financial bone in my life (Ezek. 37:4, 7, 10): Hear the word of the Lord you dry bones. Thus says the Lord to every seed that I have sown: "I will cause an abundance of life to come into you, and you shall multiply exceedingly and bring forth an unusual harvest for my child."

No promise of God must remain dead in my life. Lord you have given unto me exceedingly great and precious promises (2 Pet. 1:4). You are not a man that you should lie. Lord you said: *Give and it shall be given unto me good measure pressed down, shaken together and running over shall men give into my bosom* (paraphrased, Lk. 6:38). Therefore, I prophesy a "pressed down, shaken together and running over" blessing into my life, and into my family's life. I prophesy that my barns are filled with plenty and that my wine press shall now burst forth with an abundance of new wine. I prophesy that the windows of heaven are now opened up to me, and that so much is released to me that there is not enough room to receive it.

I declare that I have been redeemed from the curse of the law, and therefore, I prophesy that the blessings of Abraham must come upon me now according to Gal. 3:13-14. Father You blessed Abraham; You made his name great and made him a blessing, so that through him all families of the earth are still being blessed. Now, Your word says that I am blessed with faithful Abraham (Gal. 3:9) and that I am Abraham's seed, and heir according to the promise (Gal. 3:29). Abraham was very rich in livestock, silver and gold (Gen. 13:2); therefore I prophecy great possessions, property and money into my life, goal and silver in abundance.

I activate my many seeds. Let them all come together like Ezekiel's dry bones and bring me a massive harvest. I prophesy that the seed I have sown this week, combined with others that I have already sown, have caused my rain clouds to be full and bursting forth. These clouds are now emptying themselves into my life (Eccl. 11:3).

I also prophesy to every person for whose salvation I have been praying. Now is the hour for you to be saved. Turn to Jesus now!

20

Deliverance Tuesday

Today I will focus on the power associated with deliverance from financial bondage. I recognize that part of my problem is linked to spirits of financial bondage that have negatively impacted me and my family lineage over the years. I believe that the seeds that I have been sowing in the Kingdom have made a way for me to break the stranglehold of the spirit of poverty over my life.

My Declarations

In the name of Jesus, I command every generational curse in my life to be broken. What God created me for I must come into now, for He says: "I know the thoughts that I think toward you ... thoughts of peace and not of evil, to give you a future and a hope" (Jer. 29:11). I renounce the sins of my forefathers and dissociate myself from every one of their evil practices. None of their curses must affect me any more. Money and property must come into my hands and stay with me. There must be no more bags with holes receiving my money. Every leaking cistern is stopped, now!

Whatever I put my hands to do it shall prosper. My harvest shall no longer be elusive, but I shall be like a tree planted by the rivers of waters bringing forth my fruit in its seasons; my leaves also shall no longer wither (Ps. 1).

Whatever poverty stigmas have been associated with my family lineage for years now, today I pronounce them null and void. I renounce every evil practice of my parents and foreparents that may have caused a perpetuation of poverty in my family. I dissociate myself from every such practice and refuse to come under the banner of any. Jesus has brought me into His banqueting house, and His banner over me is love.

I am delivered from the snare of the fowler. I refuse to live in scarcity, for the earth is the Lord's and its fullness thereof. Since my hands are clean and my heart is pure, and I have remembered the Lord my God, I am now qualified to go into the hill of the Lord and receive the blessing from the Lord. Because I seek your face, Lord, the blessings are mine. Jesus you have come to bring deliverance to the captives, therefore I shall no longer be captive to the spirit of poverty. I choose to live life more abundantly.

Let my unsaved family members, my coworkers, my neighbors and my friends see me now in my prosperity and know and acknowledge that I am blessed of the Lord; and let them turn to you oh Lord. Replace every evil assignment over them with your divine assignment.

21

Wisdom Wednesday

Today, I will listen for the voice of wisdom, for she has come to bring me riches and honor, enduring riches and righteousness. Her fruit is better than fine gold and her revenue is better than choice silver. She will traverse my pathway of righteousness today to cause me to inherit wealth and fill my treasuries (Prov. 8:18-21). I am prepared to do whatever wisdom instructs me to do.

My Declarations

By the Spirit of wisdom, I declare that enduring riches and righteousness are with me right now and my treasury is being filled with wealth (Prov. 8:18, 21). I love wisdom and pursue her diligently; therefore, I am inheriting wealth through her right now. Her *proceeds are better than the profits of silver and her gain than fine gold. She is more precious than rubies and all the things I desire cannot compare with her. Length of days are in her right hand, in her left hand riches and honor.* (Prov. 3:14-16). Therefore, through wisdom, I am rich and honorable.

By wisdom, I rule over every aspect of my finances and decree that all that the locust, the canker worm, the palmer worm and the caterpillar have devoured of my possession is now being restored sevenfold (Prov. 8:15; Prov. 6:30-31; Joel 2:25).

I decree that my house is being built right now through wisdom; it is being established by understanding and the rooms are being filled with all precious and pleasant riches by my knowledge in the Lord (Prov. 24:3-4). Lord let me always fear you and have the deepest respect for you, so that wisdom would always accompany me, for the fear of the Lord is the beginning of wisdom (Prov. 9:10). Remove pride and arrogance from me, oh Lord, so that wisdom would love me and remain with me (Prov. 8:13).

Because I have remembered the Lord my God, He has given me the power of wisdom to get wealth. I will listen to the voice of wisdom, hear her instructions and keep her ways. I will watch daily at her gates, find life, obtain favor from the Lord and be blessed (Prov. 8:32-36). I am most blessed and highly favored of the Lord (Ps. 21:6; Lk. 1:28).

Lord, show your wisdom to all my unsaved loved ones. Let them see your glory and be saved, oh Lord.

22

Awesome Thursday

Today I will concentrate and meditate on the awesome power of God in causing me to obtain wealth. Marvelous and awesome are his works. I believe Him today that His mighty power shall be released upon my seed right now, for He does awesome things.

My Declarations

This is my day for God to do awesome things with My seed. I believe that the supernatural, omnipotent and awesome power of God is being released to bring me incredible riches right now. Just like the patriarchs Abraham, Isaac and Jacob, I shall be very rich. My God You shall respond to my seed with awesome deeds in righteousness, for your paths drip with abundance (Ps. 65:5, 11). I shout joyfully to God, sing out the honor of His name, and make His praise glorious. How awesome are His works! (Ps. 66:1-3a). Because of the greatness of your power, oh Lord, money and possessions shall submit themselves to You and be made available to me, Your servant. Father, let men see the awesome works which You are doing through Your humble servant (Ps. 66:1-5).

Lord You have tested me; You have refined me as silver is refined. You had caused men to

134

ride over my head for a short while. You had taken me through the fire and I was not consumed; and through the waters, and I was not overwhelmed; but now You are bringing me out into my wealthy place (Ps. 66:10-12). I give You praise for being so privileged.

Lord I remember Your marvelous works which You have already done, and anticipate even greater miracles today (1 Chron. 16:12). I sing unto You a new song, for You have already done marvelous things for me. Your right hand and Your holy arm have won You the victory and wrought deliverance for me (Ps. 98:1). I declare that this is the Lord's doing; it is marvelous in our eyes (Ps. 118:23). This is the day that the Lord has made; I will rejoice and be glad in it (v. 24). Save now, oh Lord; send now prosperity unto Your servant (v. 25).

Also, let an awesome work of salvation be done in my unsaved family members, my friends, neighbors and co-workers, now.

23

Dominion Friday

Today I am going to exercise my restored dominion over the earth, over my circumstances, over my finances, over every situation. Because I have sown my seed and remembered the Lord my God, He has given me the rights to take dominion over every obstacle surrounding my money matters, so that I can obtain Kingdom wealth.

My Declarations

I was born for dominion; this is my heritage as God's highest creation (Gen. 1:26). My dominion that was lost in Adam is now restored in Christ. Because I have remembered the Lord, I am the head and not the tail; I am above only and not beneath (Deut. 28). Therefore money is not my master; I am the master of money.

Money, you are my servant. Whatever I desire you to do you shall do, so that God can fulfill the covenant in me which He swore to my fathers. You are not to control me; I am in control of you instead. Because of what I have to do for God in the earth, you must be available to me in abundance. You are part of my God-ordained heritage. So you cannot be a stranger, with mere visitor status in my life anymore.

I take authority over every thief of my finances. I must have life more abundantly. I declare that I operate in the realm of the "come-upon-me-and-the-overtake-me" blessings (Deut. 28:2) as well as the "exceedingly abundantly" (Eph. 3:20). I am blessed in the city; I am blessed in the country. The fruit of my body (my children) are blessed, as well as the produce of my ground. My basket and my kneading bowl are also blessed. I am blessed coming in and blessed going out (Deut. 28:3-6). The blessing of the Lord makes (one) rich and He adds no sorrow with it (Prov. 10:22).

Dominion power is with my seed now; the more I sow into the Kingdom is the more I dominate money, the mammon of unrighteousness (Lk. 16:9, 11). Money will not dictate what I do for God or what I do in my life. I do what God would have me do in the earth and money shall be my servant to help me accomplish it.

Because I am sowing, I declare that I am at the top of my field; I am at the cutting edge of whatever I do. My services are of the highest quality and in great demand; my products are first class and irresistible. My clientele is expanding beyond my wildest dreams. Where there is the opportunity for promotion, I shall be the first to be promoted, for the earth and all who dwell therein belong to my Father; promotion comes from Him.

I have power (*exousia or authority*) to tread upon serpents and upon scorpions and over all

137

the power (*dunamis, confined and limited power*) of the enemy (Lk. 10:19). I therefore dominate every foul spirit that has been interfering with my finances and the acquisition of property, now! All the years that the canker worm, the palmer worm, the caterpillar and the locust have devoured must be restored to me now, sevenfold (Prov. 6:30-31). Enough is enough. My parents and my ancestors suffered great loss because they did not acknowledge and subject themselves in obedience to the Father, but not so with me. I declare that I am changing the very landscape of my family lineage. I shall not be poor anymore, for I now dominate the spirits of poverty and lack.

I also take dominion over the evil spirits that stand in the way of the salvation of my relatives and other acquaintances. These people must be saved. I take dominion over the spirit of barrenness. Satan you cannot hold them back any more from coming into the Kingdom. Lord let them also see me in my prosperity, acknowledge that I am blessed and turn their lives over to you.

24

Productivity Saturday

After an entire week of declarations over my seed, I expect to see tangible signs of progress today. I expect my seeds to germinate and bring forth fruit in abundance. I expect all barrenness associated with my finances to give way to fruitfulness. I have sown into fertile soil and therefore I expect nothing less than tangible results. I am result-oriented and God will not hold back any good thing from me, because I walk uprightly (Ps. 84:11b).

My Declarations

I take no counsel from the ungodly, nor do I stand where sinners stand, nor do I sit in the seat of the scornful. But Lord, I delight in your law day and night and meditate therein. Therefore, I speak productivity over my life. I declare that since my seeds are planted in well-watered soil, they shall all develop into productive trees. They shall bring forth their fruit over several seasons. Therefore, there shall be no withering of my finances anymore. I declare that abundance of prosperity be mine now; I claim this in the name of Jesus (Ps. 1:1-3). Whatever I put my hands to do it shall prosper.

I break forth into singing and cry aloud, as you command me, oh Lord. I reject barrenness and embrace productivity. I shall no longer be desolate. By faith, I enlarge the place of my tent and extend the boundaries of my dwellings with no reservations whatsoever. I lengthen my cords and strengthen my stakes, for I anticipate expanding to the right and to the left (Isa. 54:1-3, *paraphrased*).

Because I have remembered the Lord my God, I know that I shall not be put to shame. The embarrassments of the past are long gone; they shall not return. I am moving from glory to glory. The path of the just is like a shining light that is ever increasing in brightness unto the perfect day. The God I serve He is the Lord of hosts and my Redeemer (Isa. 54:4-5). No weapon formed against me shall prosper and every tongue which rises against me in judgment I shall condemn.

This is my day of jubilee, and I cause my trumpet to sound everywhere I go. My land shall yield its fruit and I shall eat in abundance and dwell there in safety (Lev. 25:19). What God intended for me to have from the beginning, I take it now. I return to my possession, for this is my right in this year of jubilee (Lev. 25:8-13). Lord I believe that you have commanded a blessing upon me that is capable of bringing forth produce for many years to come, for the wealth of the sinner is being transferred to me now, and I shall leave an inheritance for my children's children (Prov. 13:22). I declare that all my children shall be saved and forever blessed of the Lord.

25

Have You Commanded
Your Morning?

*By operating in such kingly anointing on a daily basis,
you will avert mishaps and disasters in your
life, cause your day to spring forth with joy,
and nothing shall happen to you
by chance any more.*

In this chapter, I open up one of the most potent revelations that God has made known to the last day church—commanding your morning. In the book of Job, God asks a very startling question which could have much bearing on the ultimate release of our wealth and determine our general well being, notwithstanding all that we have discussed so far:

Have you commanded the morning since your days begun, so that you put the dawn in its place, that it might take hold of the ends of the earth, and the wicked be shaken out of it? (Job 38:12-13).

We must remember that there are wicked forces that will seek to hold back our finances even if we have done everything right. Remember that the Bible says that "the wealth of the wicked is laid up for the just" (Prov. 13:22). Naturally, we expect Satan to try to hold on to this wealth and prevent the people of God from getting it. His wicked spirits will do so by latching themselves unto the dawn and manipulating it, so that we do not get what our day is supposed to bring forth for us.

Consider Daniel, a powerful intercessor and mighty prophet of God. In Daniel chapter 9, we read that his prayers were hindered for twenty-one days by the "prince" and "kings" of Persia. These were titles given to the wicked principalities operating in the second heaven above the kingdom of Persia in Daniel's day. It should be noted here that there are three heavens: (i) the atmospheric heaven (just above us, where the clouds and the rain originate—Deut. 11:17; 28:12; Judges 5:4; Acts 14); (ii) The second heaven (the starry or stellar heaven or outer space—Ps. 8:3; 19:4, 6; Jer. 8:2; Isa. 3:10); and (iii) The third heaven (God's dwelling place—1 Kgs. 8:30; Ps. 2:4; Matt. 5:16; 1 Kgs. 8:27; Deut. 10:14).

From the study of the Scriptures, it is generally understood that the second heaven is the region where wicked spirits dwell, namely, "principalities and powers in the heavenly places" (Eph. 3:10), or "spiritual hosts of wickedness in the heavenly places" (Eph. 6:12); and "the rulers of the darkness of this age." They seek to control the earth and perpetuate evil and its consequences. Evil men and women act as agents of these wicked spirits on the earth. They are the ones assigned to ensure that darkness and wickedness prevail in the earth by manipulating the dawn and transferring the evil of the night into our day.

Have You Commanded the Morning Since Your Days Begun?

The word "command" has several meanings. Among them are these: *to order, to mandate, to master, to take control of, to take authority over, to decree or declare.* When you command your morning, therefore, you exercise the right to order what takes place during the rest of the day, or you may mandate certain things to happen; then too, by commanding the morning, you may exercise mastery over every potentially detrimental circumstance that might have been earmarked to take place in your day. Or, you may take control of your day and ensure that nothing contrary intrudes into it. The Scripture says in Job 22:38: "You will also decree a thing and it will be established for you, so light will shine on your way."

By operating in such kingly anointing on a daily basis, you will avert mishaps and disasters in your life, cause your day to spring forth with joy, and nothing shall happen to you by chance any more. You will set limitations on Satan's dark practices, so that the dark deeds of the night are not transferred into your day.

In the light of the foregoing, Jesus makes what I consider to be one of the most profound statements in all of Scripture:

> *Therefore, do not worry about tomorrow, for tomorrow will worry about its own things. Sufficient for the day is its own trouble* (KJV: **"Sufficient unto the day is the evil thereof"**).

This statement seems to suggest that each day's evil has to be reprogrammed. That is, Satan assigns a quota of evil for each successive day. That is why Jesus advises that those who would trust in Him need not worry about what is going to happen tomorrow because He would see to it, as long as they work with Him, that He intercepts the evil assigned to tomorrow, and bring peace and blessings into their tomorrow. That is related to the Scriptural truth: "Weeping may endure for a night, but joy comes in the morning" (Ps. 30:5).

It is a known fact that just past midnight, during the third and forth watches of the night, until around the dawn period, or thereabout, the occult world is abuzz with activities. It's like business time for witches, warlocks, diviners, enchanters, satan worshippers, as they engage in incantations and invocations, séances, blood sacrifices, casting spells, hexes, spitting curses, and other witchcraft operations. They invoke the rulers of the darkness, and masters of spiritual wickedness to assist them in their deadly practices. This is the time when they lay their "cockatrice" eggs, and "weave the spider's web." Isaiah tells us that "he who eats of their eggs dies" (Isa. 59:4-5).

And caused the dawn to know its place

This clause suggests that the dawn is being misused, abused, manipulated or exploited by wicked forces. What is the purpose of the dawn? We all know that the dawn is that period of the day that signals the coming in of physical light to replace the darkness of the night. Therefore the dawn speaks of the ushering of productive, progressive and prosperous activities. The other expression for dawn is "dayspring" or the spring of the day, that is, when the daylight first springs forth. Spiritually speaking, one gets deep insight into the purpose of the dawn in Zecharias' statement about Jesus, the Dayspring or Dawn Himself from on high who has visited us: "To give light to those who sit in darkness and the shadow of death, to guide our feet into the way of peace" (Lk. 1:79).

The dawn, therefore, will naturally be a menace to Satan and his cohorts who are masters of darkness. They are creatures of darkness that are constantly rebelling against the light (Job 24:13). They do not want light; they want the morning to be "the same as the shadow of death; if someone recognizes them, they are in the terrors of the shadow of death" (Job. 24:17). That confirms why sinful men prefer darkness to light; their deeds are evil and shameful.

To satanic agents, the dawn then would be crucial for the transfer of the evil eggs "hatched" by them during their nocturnal operations. Strategically, the dawn would have to be viewed as a type of transshipment point for Satan and his agents. They must use it to transfer their wicked deeds of the night into the day. Satan's aim is to cloud or darken our day with his pollutions by ordering sinful, negative and detrimental effects to characterize our day. Thus the progress and prosperity that are designated to come to us via daylight are often frustrated by the spiritual opposition set up by Satan and his cohorts. By manipulating and misusing the dayspring, Satan seeks to cross the very boundaries that God has set, and in the process, severely hamper the progress of God's people. Job gives us some insight on this in Job 24:1-2ff:

Since times are not hidden from the Almighty, why do those who know Him see not His days? Some remove landmarks. They seize flocks violently and feed on them ...

The dayspring is a logical starting point for the assignment of the evil programmed for any particular day, since by the *law of first mention*, whatever is declared then, and remains unchallenged, would hold for the rest of the day. This is why the dawn is so crucial to the workers of iniquity, as well as to us the children of light. Satan knows the strategic importance of starting at the source of a thing to influence that thing. We as God's people must learn this and learn it quickly. Jesus rightly says: "for the sons of this world are more shrewd than the sons of light" (Lk. 16:8).

The above principle of influencing something at the source is not that difficult to understand. Let us use the analogy of a river. If one wants to poison the entire course of a river, one would not go some where downstream to do so; a great part of the river would not be influenced. One would instead go to the source or headspring of the river itself so that the influence would be pervasive. Or, let us consider the initial stage of a modern-day war; the first thing that the war strategist would seek to do is to knock out the nerve center or the communicative system of the enemy. Or, where one is attempting to kill a tree, the most apt point to do so would be the root, not the branches. If you go for the branches, you would most likely waste your energy, for more branches would eventually proliferate where one branch is removed. However, once the root is detached or poisoned, the entire tree, as big as it is, would soon wither and topple over.

Indeed, that is why the evil one finds the dawn or the dayspring so attractive. The dayspring signals light; Satan, as we know, rebels against light. What he wants is for men to live in darkness. Thus once he gets his grip on the spring of the day, he would pollute it and rob our day of what it was intended to yield for us. The believers in Christ are the only ones to stop him from polluting our waters, so to speak; we must not allow darkness to pervade the face of the deep anymore. We must be in position to say, "Let there be light," by commanding our morning and allowing the dawn to know its place.

How significant is the truth that Jesus is the Dayspring from on high, in the light of all that we have been discussing? If Jesus is the Dayspring, then He is the one that ushers in the day, spiritually speaking, not Satan and his rebellious crew. The truth is that we are joint-heirs with Christ, and therefore we are expected to partner with Him in ensuring that what God intended the day to bring forth for us from the beginning, it indeed brings forth. All the blessings and inheritance that are due to God's people for each day would be guaranteed if we can partner with the Dayspring (or Dawn) Himself at the dayspring hour. Neither Satan nor the spiritual hosts of wickedness in the heavenly places can withstand such a combined force. Remember that Jesus Himself tells us "that if two of you agree on earth concerning anything that they ask, it shall be done for them by my Father in heaven" (Matt.18:19). Only this time we are agreeing with the Dayspring Himself at the dayspring hour. What a phenomenon!

We have first rights to the dawn. The Holy Spirit revealed to me that by virtue of the fact that the dawn signals the approaching light, we, the children of light, have first rights to the dawn, not the evil one. However, if we fail to capitalize on our rights, we leave room for the wicked one to take the initiative and bring darkness into our day instead. Consequently, we allow ourselves to lose by default. Then we have ourselves to blame for whatever happens later in the day.

Now let us return to Job 38:12-13:

Have you commanded the morning since your days begun, so that you put the dawn in its place, that it might take hold of the ends of the earth, and the wicked be shaken out of it?

We have a mandate to put the dawn in its place, for the wicked spirits seek to abuse, misuse or misapply it. They have been exploiting the dawn for their own purpose. God wants us to command the morning so that the dawn is put in its rightful place or to its proper use.

Prophetic Word

The Holy Spirit will say to us now: *This is the time for positioning and timing in your warfare against the enemy. The days for brute-force tactics are long gone; the days for matching the enemy stride for stride in the valley are over. Position yourself at the spring of the river, at the top of everything, at the spring of your day. Now is the time for efficient and effective engagement of the forces of darkness—strategic level warfare. At the dayspring, Satan and his dark creatures are just about trying to manipulate the dawn to control your day. The evil spirits are not yet let out of their dark holes to pervade the earth for the day.*

Thus says the Lord: *It is easier to block the mouth of the cave rather that wait until the lions are let out to then try to control each one separately. If our timing and positioning is right, in effect, there would be no real warfare. The Dayspring from on high has already won the victory for us on the cross. What we should be doing is simply taking the victory, not fighting for the victory; Satan cannot really put up a fight with you if you are fighting at the dawn. I, Your God, have already given you superior power or exousia to tread upon serpents and scorpions, and over all the power of the enemy; now I give you positioning and timing. You have a virtually unbeatable position; you cannot lose. You are more than conquerors indeed.*

Hear My word: *The more wicked the enemy gets, the easier I'll make it for you to defeat him. You will not have to use brute-force tactics against Satan. I will show you how to match his latest schemes by causing you to knock out nerve centers and communication systems. I will show you how to blow up spiritual bridges, cut off the enemy, and leave him stranded, without one diabolical agent or evil spirit being able to raise his sword. Where sin would seem to abound, my grace will much more abound*, says the Lord.

That it might take hold of the ends of the earth

What amazing revelation! This is clearly one of the most potent revelations for the last day church. Can you imagine this kind of power being available to God's people now? Let us use it to our great advantage, for His glory and our victory. The word "ends" also means "edges." It seems that the dawn, when operating in its correct perspective, has widespread influence over everything. It can take hold of the corners of our personal lives, our households, our neighborhoods, our communities, our nation and any nation or peoples to which our decrees and declarations are directed.

And the wicked be shaken out of it

Here is proof that the wicked seek to latch themselves unto the dawn in an effort to manipulate it. But once the dawn is in place, it has the power to shake the wicked from itself. In other words, the dawn has a self-cleansing ability. Indeed, the Father gives a strange assignment to the dawn. This is very mysterious language, but God Himself is speaking, so we have to pay careful attention to what is being said. What stupendous mystery! How this works is not for us to conjecture; all we need to do is to be actively involved in prayer and declarations at the dayspring and see the marvelous, unbelievable things that God would do as a result. There are different dimensions of the impact. Simply by commanding your morning, the wicked, thieving spirits can be shaken off from the edges of our personal lives, our community and the nation as a whole.

When should we command the morning?

Now, there is no way we can cause the dawn to know its place if we rise up from our sleep after dawn has passed. To command our morning, therefore, we must rise before dawn (most commonly recognized as between the hours of 5.00 a.m. and 6.00 a.m.), and ensure that we set the stage for those good and perfect gifts that come down from the Father of lights (James 1:17). We must take the opportunity to make positive declarations, based on the word of God, over our personal lives, our family, our neighborhood, our community and our nation as a whole. That's also the most ideal vantage point where we can effectively apply the blood of Jesus so that it could saturate the entire day and bring about the cleansing to which the Scriptures refer. All believers should be up and praying at this time, so that we could say to the enemy and his dark spirits: "So far and no more." We ought to ensure that the legitimate spiritual boundaries or landmarks are not removed by the evil one, as Job tells us (Job 24:1-2), and that his darkness is not transferred to our day.

In our church, we now do the "dayspring" prayer service (5.00 a.m. to 6.00a.m.) every single day (including Sundays), since God brought the revelation to us at the end of June, 2007. It is one of our biggest prayer meetings, and growing stronger. It is one of the most glorious prayer and intercessory experiences that we have had in recent times. We have been using these mornings to speak many things into our ministry, our personal lives, our communities and our nation as a whole. Through this route, we are confident that we have been able to cancel many predictions of darkness and national disasters that have been made from time to time by psychics and diviners over Trinidad and Tobago.

Can you think of a better time to make your daily Kingdom wealth declarations (chapters 17 to 23) than early in the morning during the dawn? Whatever we say then must carry maximum impact. When it comes to Kingdom wealth, once we have paid our tithes and sown our seed, we would see our harvest come to us in abundance.

This phenomenon certainly has great potential for our financial breakthroughs, among other things, since the thief who comes to steal, to kill and to destroy would often try to put a stranglehold on our finances. By commanding our morning and causing the dawn to know its place, we have the power to shake that "devourer" out of the dawn, so that the dayspring ushers in blessings not curses. The wicked one can no longer keep our finances in bondage, once we begin to command our morning, since he is shaken out of it. What a phenomenon! Command your morning! Command your morning! In the final analysis, when we combine the wealth principles taught in this book with the practice of commanding our morning, success seems inevitable, to say the least.

I believe that in this book we have explored every possible avenue to enable the average believer in Christ to get wealth. The only way that one may not realize the inevitable benefits is if there is inconsistency of effort and dishonesty towards God. As long as one follows the instructions diligently and earnestly, one will be on the way to getting the blessing that makes rich and adds no sorrow with it. You would not need the lottery, or any get-rich-quick scheme. There will be no remorse or negative repercussions from dishonest and unlawful gain, for there will be no need for doing anything unlawful to succeed. What you receive as wealth will be totally your heritage from the Lord as an heir of God and joint-heir with Jesus Christ. What a day for God's people! Go forth and take all the wealth being offered by God, with no reservations whatsoever. Hallelujah!

REFERENCE LIST

Brown, Francis, S.R. Driver, Charles A. Briggs. 1992. *Hebrew and English lexicon of the Old Testament.* Grand Rapids: Zondervan.

Soanes, Catherine et al (eds.). 2005. *Pocket Oxford English Dictionary (10th ed.).* Oxford: Oxford University Press.

ISBN 142515182-5

9 781425 151829

Edwards Brothers Malloy
Oxnard, CA USA
`oril 4, 2013